JENNIFER ANISTON
Cook with Clydeo

A COOKBOOK FOR KIDS

HARPER
An Imprint of HarperCollinsPublishers

Cook with Clydeo: A Cookbook for Kids
Copyright © 2025 by Invisible Universe Inc.
All rights reserved. Manufactured in Johor, Malaysia.
No part of this book may be used or reproduced in any manner whatsoever
without written permission except in the case of brief quotations embodied
in critical articles and reviews. For information address
HarperCollins Children's Books, a division of
HarperCollins Publishers, 195 Broadway, New York, NY 10007.
www.harpercollinschildrens.com

Library of Congress Control Number: 2024944511
ISBN 978-0-06-337238-2

Interior design by Georgia Rucker Design
Production management by Stonesong
Recipe development by Coco Morante
Clydeo animation stills by Invisible Universe Inc.
Food photography by Dana Gallagher except the below:

Shutterstock/Formatoriginal, pp. vi–vii; Shutterstock/Joe Gough, p. 15; Shutterstock/grey_and, p. 16, p. 44; Shutterstock/baibaz, p. 20, p. 73, p. 97; Shutterstock/NataliaZa, p. 24, p. 47; Shutterstock/Melica, p. 27; Shutterstock/Khumthong, p. 28, 31; Shutterstock/Niradj, p. 34; Shutterstock/Ermak Oksana, p.38; Shutterstock/Nataly Studio, p. 40; Shutterstock/Moving Moment, p. 43; Shutterstock/exopixel, p. 48 (green peppers); Shutterstock/Eywa (red peppers), p. 48; Shutterstock/MaraZe, p. 51; Shutterstock/xpixel, p. 54 (top); Shutterstock/Collins Unlimited, p. 54 (bottom); Shutterstock/Hong Vo, p. 57; Shutterstock/PhotoMavenStock, p. 58; Shutterstock/GSDesign, p. 61; Shutterstock/anat chant, p. 65; Shutterstock/Tiger Images, p. 66 (top); Shutterstock/Shahril KHMD, p. 66 (bottom); Shutterstock/penguin, p. 70; Shutterstock/BW Folsom, p. 74; Shutterstock/Tim UR, p. 76, p. 84; Shutterstock/Andrei Dubadzel, p. 82 (top); Shutterstock/Sergey Sklezenev, p. 82 (bottom); Shutterstock/Natdanai99, p. 92; Shutterstock/Dreamsquare, p. 92 (bottom right); Shutterstock/yulyamade, p. 94 (top); Shutterstock/Yeti studio, p. 94 (bottom), p. 106; Shutterstock/Sergiy Kuzmin, p. 98; Shutterstock/studiovin, p. 100 (top); Shutterstock/Diana Taliun, p. 100 (bottom); Shutterstock/Sarah Marchant, p. 114; Shutterstock/Ian 2010, p. 118

Products, trademarks, and trademark names are used in this
book to describe and inform the reader about various proprietary
products that are owned by third parties. No endorsement of
the information contained in this book is given by the owners of
such products and trademarks and no endorsement is implied
by the inclusion of product or trademarks in this book.

25 26 27 28 29 PCA 10 9 8 7 6 5 4 3 2 1
FIRST EDITION

When cooking, it is important to keep safety in mind. Children should always ask permission from an adult before cooking and should be supervised by an adult in the kitchen at all times.

SUPER IMPORTANT!
These are recipes for my human family, not my dog family.
Some of these ingredients can make real dogs very sick,
so save them for your people friends and family!

Love, Clydeo

CONTENTS

vi INTRODUCTION

2 BREAKFAST

- **4** Finger-Lickin' French Toast Skewers
- **8** Fruit-Topped Crepes & Chocolate Sauce
- **12** Breakfast Quesadilla
- **16** Scrumptious Shakshuka
- **20** Banana Pancake Bites
- **24** Cozy Oatmeal Banana Splits
- **28** Loaded Breakfast Burgers

32 LUNCH

- **34** Crunchy Apple, Cheddar & Chicken Salad
- **36** Thai-Inspired Peanut Noodle Salad
- **38** Chicken Caesar Pasta Salad
- **40** Cheesy & Beefy Pasta
- **44** The Coziest Chicken & Tortellini Soup
- **48** DIY Pizza Bar

52 DINNER

54 Clydeo's Legendary Lasagna

58 Tasty Turkey Meatball Subs

62 Taco 'Bout a Good Burger

66 Handmade Sweet Potato Gnocchi

70 Chicken & Vegetable Fried Rice

74 Loaded Hot Dog Bar

76 Pot Roast French Dip Sandwiches

80 SNACKS & SIDES

82 Queso Dip

84 Very Berry Smoothie

86 Jennifer Aniston's Easy Enchilada Bites

90 Mini Bruschetta Bites

92 Healthy & Hearty Homemade Hummus

94 How to Build a Charcuterie & Cheese Board

98 Toast, but Make It Pizza!

100 Sweet Potato Nachos

102 DESSERTS & DOG TREAT

104 No-Bake Oreo Pie

106 You'll Want S'more, S'mores Dip

108 Funfetti Cookies

110 Caramel Apple Pretzel Bites

112 Scrumptious Strawberry & Cheesecake Ice Cream Sandwiches

114 No-Bake Crispy Rice Peanut Butter Bars

118 4-Ingredient Homemade Dog Treats

Hi!

I'm Clydeo. Dog, companion, and best friend of Jennifer Aniston. Her dog Clyde is my cousin. You might be wondering what a dog is doing with a cookbook. Well, food is my life! And I've been sharing my recipes on the internet for years now as my dreams of becoming the most famous furry foodie are underway. I love cooking for friends and family and planning my next food adventure. Sometimes I'll lie in bed at night and think about what I might have for breakfast the next day. And what my next snack will be. And don't forget about lunch . . . You get the picture. I've been this way ever since I was a pup. My family, the Clydes, have always loved gathering around the dinner table to share a meal, and they got their grub by befriending the owners of the best restaurants around. But I wanted to do more than just eat delicious food, I wanted to *make* delicious food. My family howled their unconditional support and helped me get to LA, the best place for a burgeoning star like me! Luckily Jen, Clyde, and Lord Chesterfield let me stay. One step closer to my dreams!

Living in LA has been a big change, and I gotta say, it's been great for a fledgling foodie and home cook like me. The city is brimming with culinary inspiration and flavors. From farmers' markets to my favorite local taco trucks, the streets are full of delicious scents that would drive any dog wild. With some encouragement from Jen, and with Clyde and Lord Chesterfield by my side to clean up any food I drop on the ground, the kitchen has become my home base and where my creativity thrives! The first dish I made was my Legendary Lasagna and . . . I burned it. Oops! But Jen just cut off the crispy edges and gave me a hug and told me to keep cooking. This was just the confidence boost I needed to keep trying new dishes. And try I did. Dips and desserts and pasta and pizza, I cooked it all. It took a lot of trial and error, but the best of my recipes are the ones I'm sharing here with you. If you're passionate about food like I am, then maybe you'll be inspired by my adventures to start cooking, too. These are some of my favorite tips to get you started in the kitchen:

- 🐾 Have everything organized before you start cooking. The French call this mise en place. Read the recipe the entire way through, then gather all your ingredients and get out any pots and pans or special equipment you need. There's nothing that makes your tail droop faster than getting halfway through a recipe only to realize you don't have any garlic.

- 🐾 Don't be afraid to make mistakes. Just like learning to shake or to roll over, cooking takes a lot of practice. There are also lots of little skills that take repetition, too. Chopping and cutting with a knife is a learned skill, as is cracking an egg and knowing when a cake is done baking. And if you think it's hard for you, be thankful that you have opposable thumbs! Don't be discouraged if you burn a few meals or spill something. Your pack will love you no matter what, and your cooking will improve over time.

- 🐾 Ask for help when you need it—especially if you're a young pup! Accidents happen when you try to reach a shelf that's too high or lean over a stove when it's hot. Jen has to open a jar for me at least once a week. Asking for help builds community, and isn't that what cooking is all about? Also, having people help and take on different tasks means you get to eat sooner, which is definitely something to bark about. Cheers to lots of delicious meals and wagging tails!

🐾 *Clydeo*

BREAKFAST

If I'm being honest, I am not the biggest fan of mornings. I'd rather snooze in a sunbeam and catch up on some beauty rest. But where there's maple syrup, there's a way! These breakfast recipes are delicious enough to rouse even the sleepiest of pups (and humans) from their slumber. Some of the dishes are quick and perfect for weekday mornings, like the Finger-Lickin' French Toast Skewers (page 4) and Breakfast Quesadilla (page 12). Others, like the Fruit-Topped Crepes & Chocolate Sauce (page 8) and Scrumptious Shakshuka (page 16), are better for weekends when you have more time and the whole family can chip in!

3 BREAKFAST

FINGER-LICKIN' FRENCH TOAST SKEWERS

Sugar, cinnamon spice, and everything nice! One of my favorite ways to start the day is on a sweet note. Little helpers can thread the bread onto the skewers and whisk up the egg mixture for this handheld breakfast.

MAKES 8 SKEWERS

PREP TIME
10 minutes

COOK TIME
5 minutes

INGREDIENTS

- Half loaf challah bread or soft French bread, about 8 ounces, cut into 1-inch cubes
- 2 large eggs
- ¾ cup whole milk
- ¼ teaspoon ground cinnamon
- Cooking oil spray, such as avocado oil

FOR SERVING

- Powdered sugar
- Maple syrup
- Blueberries and/or strawberries

5   BREAKFAST

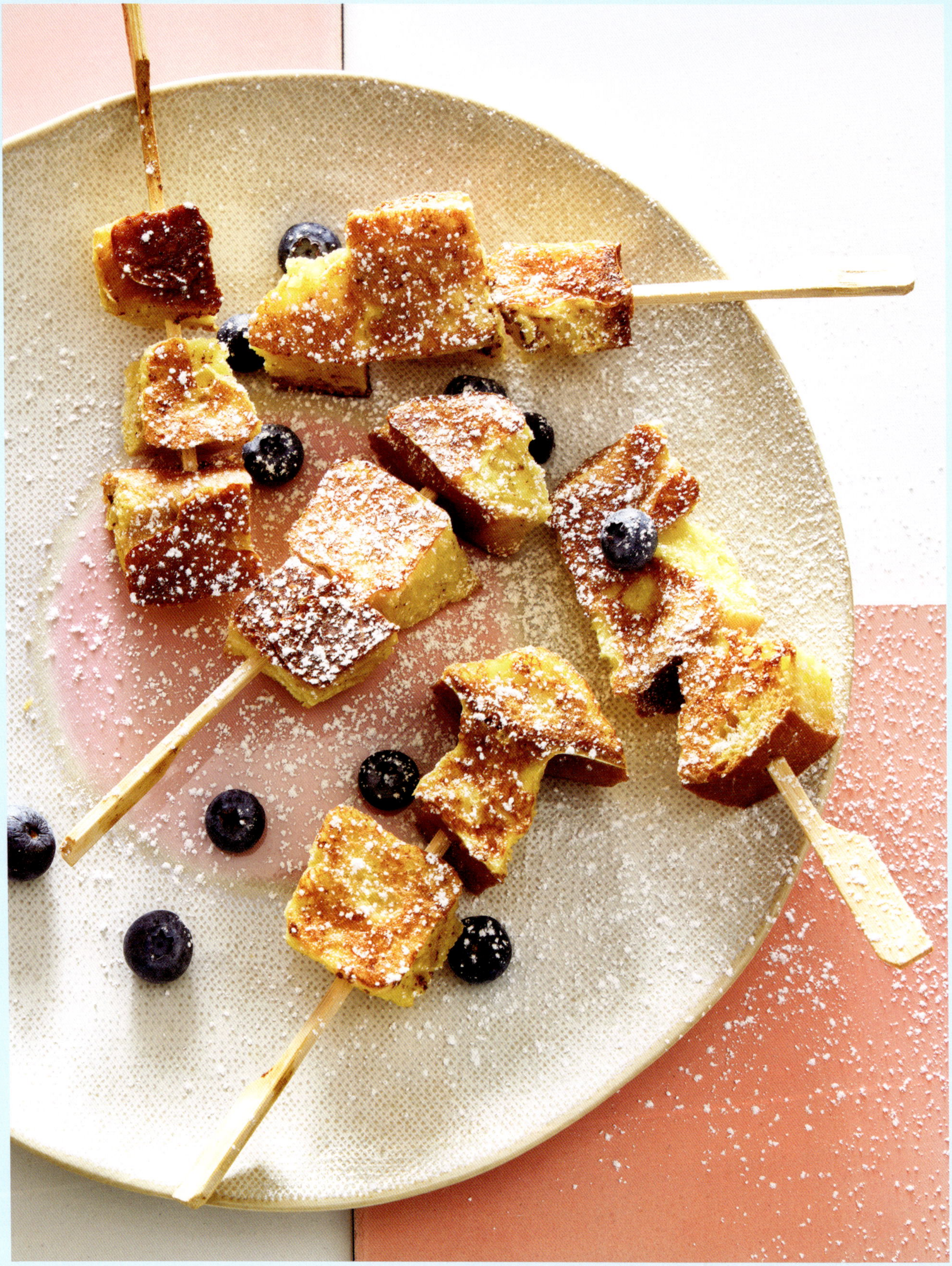

FINGER-LICKIN' FRENCH TOAST SKEWERS

DIRECTIONS

1. Preheat an air fryer to 400°F, or an oven to 425°F on its convection setting if it has one.

2. Thread the cubed bread onto eight 6-inch bamboo skewers (the flat kind with a little paddle on the end are best, for easier skewering and turning).

3. In a 9 x 13–inch baking dish, whisk together the eggs, milk, and cinnamon.

4. Add the breaded skewers to the baking dish. Let them sit in the egg mixture for about 15 seconds on each side, turning the skewers over a few times so that all sides of the bread are dipped into the egg/milk mixture.

5. Place the skewers in the preheated air fryer basket, or on a parchment-lined baking sheet in as even a layer as possible. Spray them with cooking oil, and cook for 5 minutes in the air fryer or 8 minutes in the oven, turning the skewers and spraying them again halfway through cooking. (An adult should turn the skewers, with tongs or by hand, wearing a heatproof glove.) The skewers will be golden brown and piping hot.

6. Transfer the skewers to serving plates. Sprinkle with powdered sugar and serve warm, with maple syrup and berries on the side.

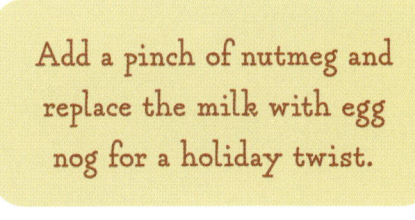

Add a pinch of nutmeg and replace the milk with egg nog for a holiday twist.

BREAKFAST

FRUIT-TOPPED CREPES & CHOCOLATE SAUCE

Use a blender to make the easy batter for these delicious crepes. They're topped with fresh fruit and drizzled with a two-ingredient chocolate sauce. I love to use strawberries, blueberries, and kiwi, but choose your favorite fruits and enjoy!

MAKES 8 CREPES

PREP TIME
5 minutes

COOK TIME
20 minutes

INGREDIENTS

FOR THE CREPES

- 1 cup whole milk
- 2 large eggs
- ½ teaspoon vanilla extract
- ¼ teaspoon kosher salt
- 1 cup all-purpose flour
- 2 tablespoons unsalted butter, melted and cooled
- More butter, for cooking the crepes

FOR THE CHOCOLATE SAUCE

- ¼ cup Nutella
- ¼ cup heavy whipping cream

FOR SERVING

- 8 strawberries, sliced
- 1 cup blueberries
- Or your favorite fruits, sliced

9 BREAKFAST

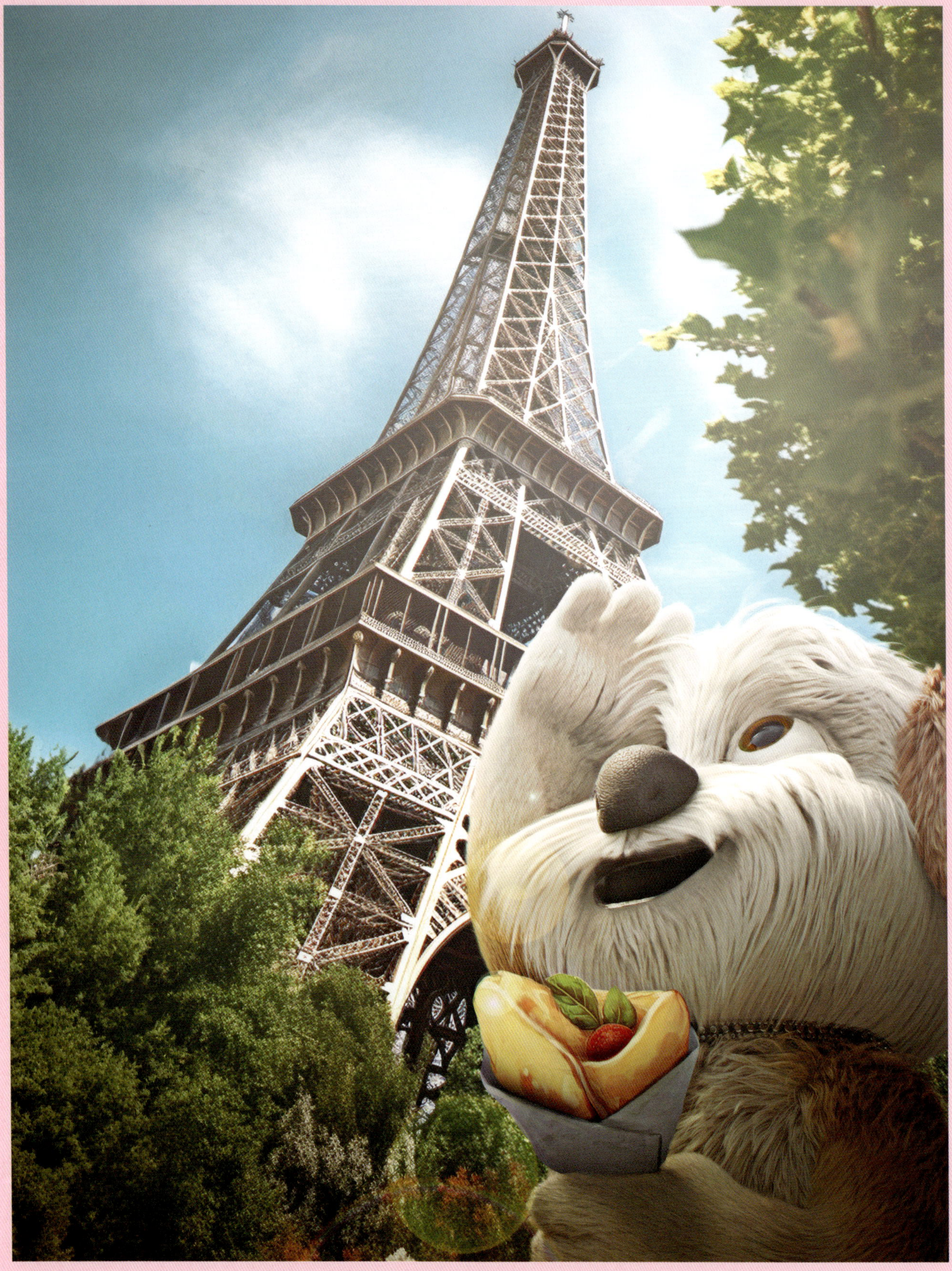

FRUIT-TOPPED CREPES & CHOCOLATE SAUCE

DIRECTIONS

1 Make the crepes: Combine the milk, eggs, vanilla, salt, and flour in a blender. Mix at low speed for about 30 seconds, adding the butter in a thin stream through the hole in the blender lid while the batter is mixing. Turn off the blender. If there is any flour on the sides, scrape down using a rubber spatula and blend at low speed for another 5 seconds or so, until all the flour is incorporated into the batter.

2 Heat a 10-inch nonstick frying pan over medium heat for 2 minutes. Add a ¼ teaspoon of butter and, using a spatula, spread it around the pan.

3 Add ¼ cup of the batter and immediately swirl it around in the pan to make an even layer. Let it cook for about 1 minute, or until the crepe is dry on top and lightly brown on the bottom. You can use a thin flexible spatula to take a peek. Flip the crepe and cook for 1 more minute on its second side. Transfer to a plate and repeat with the remaining batter. You should have a total of 8 crepes when finished.

4 Make the chocolate sauce: Warm the Nutella in a small bowl in the microwave for 20 seconds, stir, then microwave for another 10 seconds. It should be warm but not bubbling hot. Add the cream and stir until thoroughly combined. The sauce should have a thick but pourable consistency. If it is too thick, stir in a tablespoon of hot water.

5 Fold each crepe in half, then fold again to form a triangle. Place the crepes on serving plates, two to a plate, and top with the fruit and drizzle with the chocolate sauce.

NOTE For a savory variation, add a slice of ham and some grated cheddar or Swiss cheese to a warm crepe, fold into triangles, and enjoy.

BREAKFAST

BREAKFAST QUESADILLA

A fast and filling breakfast you can even eat on the go, this quesadilla is a soft flour tortilla filled with cheesy scrambled eggs and crispy bacon. I often make these in advance to store in the freezer so I always have a hearty breakfast on hand to reheat before I go out and about! They keep, frozen, for up to two months.

SERVES 1

PREP TIME
5 minutes

COOK TIME
5 minutes

INGREDIENTS

- 1 teaspoon avocado oil or other neutral oil, such as canola or vegetable oil
- 1 large egg
- Freshly ground black pepper
- ¼ cup grated cheese (Mexican cheese blend or Colby-Jack), divided
- 1 (8-inch) flour tortilla
- 1 slice crispy cooked bacon, crumbled

FOR SERVING

- Pico de gallo
- Guacamole (homemade, see page 89, or store-bought)
- Sour cream

BREAKFAST

This recipe is easily scaled up.
If you're making more than one
quesadilla, keep the finished ones
warm on a sheet pan in a 200°F oven.

BREAKFAST QUESADILLA

DIRECTIONS

1 Heat the oil in a 10-inch nonstick skillet over medium heat.

2 While the skillet is heating up, crack the egg into a small bowl and scramble with a fork.

3 Pour the egg into the pan and immediately swirl it around to make an even layer. Add a few grinds of pepper on top of the egg, sprinkle on half the cheese, then place the tortilla on top.

4 Run a thin, flexible spatula around the edges of the pan to loosen the egg, then flip the quesadilla over so that the egg layer is on top. Sprinkle the remaining cheese and the bacon over one half of the quesadilla, then fold it over.

5 Cook the folded quesadilla for about 1 minute, flip it over, and cook for an additional minute, or until both sides are golden brown.

6 Transfer the quesadilla to a plate. Slice it into wedges and serve with pico de gallo, guacamole, and/or sour cream on the side.

NOTE For heartier quesadillas, double the quantities of eggs and add bacon.

SCRUMPTIOUS SHAKSHUKA

Make sure to have lots of warm pita bread or fluffy couscous ready to go with all the yummy tomato and bell pepper sauce. The eggs are cooked until the whites are set and the yolks are just how you like them, whether that's runny (my favorite jammy eggs) or cooked all the way through.

CLYDEO'S TIPS AND TRICKS

Eggshells in your food is a big no-no. While a less-discerning dog might be willing to crunch through it, those of us with more refined palates want our eggs to be shell-free. For this, you need a small shallow bowl. Crack the egg into the bowl, inspecting it to make sure there is no shell. Once you've checked it, press the back of a large spoon or ladle into the shakshuka tomato sauce, making a nice little empty pool for your egg to nest in. Delicately tip the egg into the pool so that the yolk remains unbroken. Repeat with the remaining eggs.

SERVES 3 TO 4

PREP TIME
5 minutes

COOK TIME
15 minutes

INGREDIENTS
- 2 tablespoons olive oil
- 2 cloves garlic, chopped
- ½ medium yellow onion, chopped
- ½ teaspoon ground cumin
- ½ teaspoon kosher salt
- 2 roasted red bell peppers, chopped
- 1 (20-to-24-ounce) jar tomato passata (puree)
- 6 large eggs
- 1 tablespoon chopped fresh flat-leaf parsley

FOR SERVING
- Warm pita bread or cooked couscous (following package instructions)

BREAKFAST

18

SCRUMPTIOUS SHAKSHUKA

DIRECTIONS

1 Using a 4-quart pan with a lid, heat the olive oil and garlic over medium heat. When the garlic starts dancing in the oil, add the onion and sauté for about 3 minutes, or until the onion becomes translucent. Add the cumin and salt and sauté for another 30 seconds or so, or until the cumin is fragrant.

2 Stir in the bell peppers and the tomato passata and let it come to a simmer. One at a time, crack the eggs into the pan, spacing them out evenly in the sauce. Cover the pan, turn the heat down to medium-low, and let cook for 8 to 10 minutes, or until the whites of the eggs are set and the yolks are cooked to your liking.

3 Spoon the shakshuka into shallow serving bowls. Sprinkle with parsley and serve with pita or couscous on the side.

To spice up your shakshuka, add a diced jalapeño along with the onion and garlic, or a pinch of cayenne along with the cumin.

BREAKFAST

BANANA PANCAKE BITES

I was making silver dollar pancakes one morning when I realized they would be even better filled with banana. I started to make these bite-size flapjacks with a warm slice of banana cooked right inside—YUM! A breakfast finger food great for dipping into a pool of maple syrup, no forks required.

MAKES 48 PANCAKE BITES

PREP TIME
5 minutes

COOK TIME
20 minutes

INGREDIENTS

- 1 cup plus 2 tablespoons all-purpose flour
- 1 tablespoon granulated sugar
- 1 teaspoon baking powder
- ½ teaspoon baking soda
- ¼ teaspoon kosher salt
- 1 cup buttermilk
- 1 large egg
- 1 teaspoon vanilla extract
- 4 bananas, cut into ½-inch-thick slices (12 slices per banana)
- Cooking oil spray, such as canola or vegetable

FOR SERVING

- Maple syrup

21 BREAKFAST

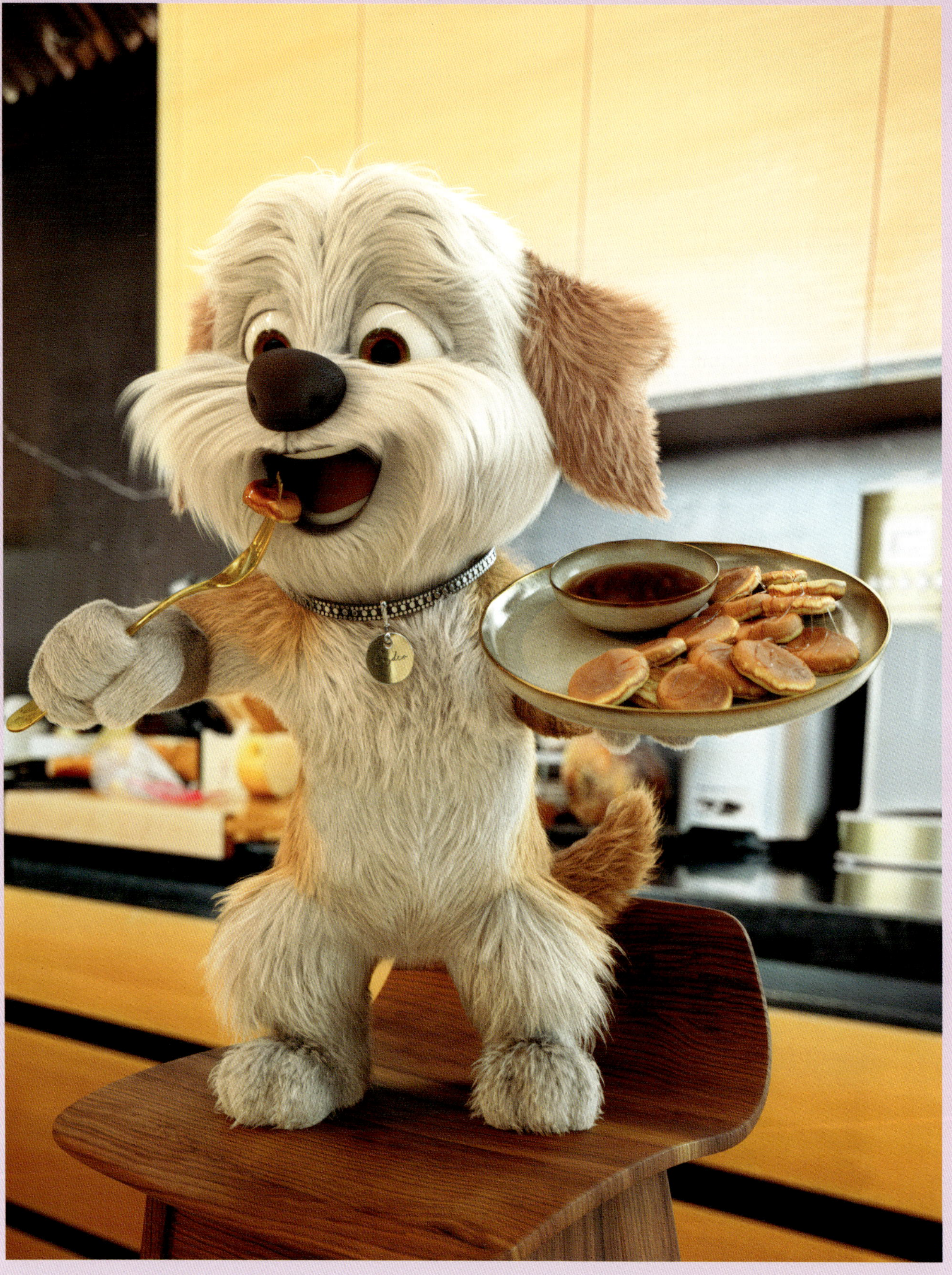

BANANA PANCAKE BITES

DIRECTIONS

1. In a medium mixing bowl, whisk together the flour, sugar, baking powder, baking soda, and salt.

2. Make a well in the center of the dry ingredients, then add the buttermilk, egg, and vanilla. Whisk the egg and vanilla into the buttermilk, then whisk the dry ingredients into the wet ingredients until all the flour is incorporated and you have a smooth, thick pancake batter.

3. Heat a 12-inch nonstick skillet over medium heat. Add 12 banana slices to the bowl of pancake batter, and use a fork to gently submerge them in the batter.

4. Spray the heated skillet with cooking oil. Using a fork, retrieve one of the banana slices from the pancake batter, give it a little shake over the bowl to let any excess batter drip off, then gently transfer it to the skillet.

5. Let the pancakes cook for about 2 minutes, or until golden brown on the bottom. Flip and cook for about 2 minutes more, or until brown on the second side and cooked through.

6. Transfer the pancakes to a serving plate. In batches of 12, repeat steps 3–6 with the remaining sliced bananas and batter until all the pancakes are cooked.

7. Serve warm with maple syrup on the side.

These are yummy dipped in chocolate sauce, too (see page 8).

BREAKFAST

COZY OATMEAL BANANA SPLITS

Banana splits for breakfast! Oatmeal takes the place of ice cream for a hearty start to the day. Whipped Greek yogurt, your favorite fruits, and a sprinkle of cacao nibs top this colorful bowl. Make sure to use bananas that are still completely yellow and firm, without any spots—they'll hold their shape when you flip them in the pan.

SERVES 2

PREP TIME
5 minutes

COOK TIME
15 minutes

INGREDIENTS

FOR THE OATMEAL

- 1 cup old-fashioned oats
- 1 cup whole milk
- ¾ cup water

FOR THE BANANAS

- 1 tablespoon coconut oil or avocado oil
- 2 ripe bananas, cut in half lengthwise
- ¼ teaspoon cinnamon

FOR THE WHIPPED GREEK YOGURT

- ½ cup plain Greek yogurt
- 2 tablespoons heavy whipping cream
- 2 tablespoons powdered sugar
- ¼ teaspoon vanilla extract

TOPPINGS

- 1 cup chopped or small fruits: strawberries, kiwis, pineapples, blueberries or raspberries, pomegranate seeds . . . whatever you like!
- 2 tablespoons cacao nibs, hemp seeds, or chopped nuts
- 1 tablespoon date syrup, honey, or agave nectar

BREAKFAST

MY BIG FAT GREEK CUISINE
THE SEA AND THE SUSHI
breakfast recipes

COZY OATMEAL BANANA SPLITS

DIRECTIONS

1 Make the oatmeal: In a 2-quart saucepan with a lid, over medium-high heat, combine the oats, milk, and water. Bring to a boil (this will take about 5 minutes), then turn the heat down to medium-low and let simmer for about 5 minutes, stirring occasionally, or until the oats have thickened and are creamy. Turn off the heat, cover, and set aside.

2 Make the bananas: Heat the coconut oil in a 10-inch skillet over medium heat. When the oil is hot, add the bananas, cut side down, and let them sear for about 2 minutes, or until golden brown. Using a thin, flexible spatula, turn the bananas, and cook them for another minute on their second side. Turn off the heat and sprinkle the bananas with the cinnamon.

3 Make the whipped Greek yogurt: In a small mixing bowl, using a whisk, whip the yogurt, heavy cream, sugar, and vanilla together for about 2 minutes, or until light and fluffy.

4 Divide the cooked oatmeal between two serving bowls. Place two banana halves on top of each bowl of oatmeal. Dollop the whipped yogurt on top, add your choice of toppings, and drizzle with the date syrup, honey, or agave nectar. Serve right away.

NOTE *My favorite oatmeal topping is peanut butter. Warm up a few tablespoons in the microwave and drizzle it on top if you like!*

BREAKFAST

LOADED BREAKFAST BURGERS

It's never too early for a burger. Sausage patties take the place of beef burgers in these breakfast-ready sandwiches. They're big and hearty, with sausage, cheese, veggies, and a fried egg on top.

SERVES 4

PREP TIME
5 minutes

COOK TIME
15 minutes

INGREDIENTS

- 4 English muffins, split in half with a fork
- 12-ounce package (8 count) breakfast sausage patties, uncooked, thawed if frozen
- 4 slices cheddar or American cheese
- 4 tablespoons aioli (garlic or sriracha)
- 4 (¼-inch-thick) slices heirloom tomato or slicing tomato
- 2 romaine lettuce leaves, cut in half crosswise
- Cooking oil spray, such as canola or vegetable
- 4 large eggs

BREAKFAST

30

LOADED BREAKFAST BURGERS

DIRECTIONS

1. Place the English muffins in a toaster. Don't turn it on yet—you'll toast them when you're ready to assemble the burgers.

2. Heat a 12-inch nonstick skillet over medium heat.

3. Using your hands, stack two of the patties together, then shape them into a 4-inch round patty. Repeat with the remaining sausage to make four patties.

4. Add the sausage patties to the skillet (no oil needed). Cook them for about 4 minutes, or until they are golden brown and turning opaque about halfway up their sides. Turn the patties and cook for about 4 more minutes, or until they're fully cooked. Turn off the heat and place a cheese slice on top of each sausage patty.

5. While the patties are cooking, toast the English muffins.

6. Place the English muffins on serving plates. Spread the top half of each muffin with 1 tablespoon aioli. Place the cheese-covered sausage patties on the bottom of each muffin, and stack a tomato slice and a piece of lettuce on top.

7. Wipe out the skillet you used to cook the sausages, then place it over medium heat once again. Spray the skillet with cooking oil, then, one at a time, break the eggs into the pan. Cook them whichever way you like (sunny-side up, over easy, etc.).

8. Slide an egg on top of the lettuce on each sandwich and, finally, cover them with the top halves of the muffin.

9. Serve right away.

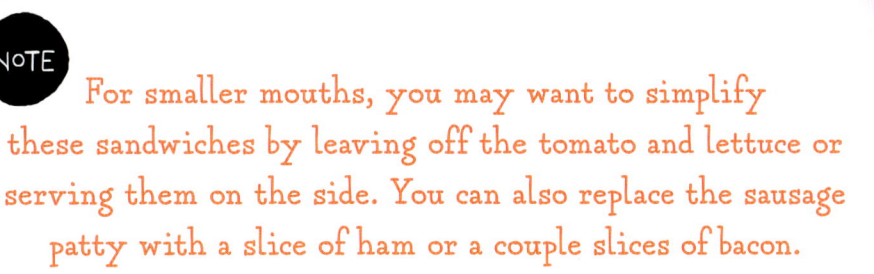

NOTE: For smaller mouths, you may want to simplify these sandwiches by leaving off the tomato and lettuce or serving them on the side. You can also replace the sausage patty with a slice of ham or a couple slices of bacon.

LUNCH

Lunch can sometimes be an overlooked meal, sandwiched (ha—sandwiched!) between its more often written about companions, breakfast and dinner. However, I love it because it gives me an opportunity to play around in the kitchen and swap ingredients and flavors. My lunch recipes are substantial enough to keep you full until dinnertime but aren't so heavy that your eyelids are dragging midway through the afternoon. Not everyone has the luxury of taking a siesta every day like me! If you are still going to obedience lessons (Jen tells me the humans just call this "school"), you might not be able to make a hot lunch. For you, I've got recipes like Thai-Inspired Peanut Noodle Salad (page 36) and Chicken Caesar Pasta Salad (page 38) that you can make the night before and pack for the days ahead. Make sure to sneak some Funfetti Cookies (page 108) into your lunch bag, too. They're like a belly rub for your soul!

33   LUNCH

CRUNCHY APPLE, CHEDDAR & CHICKEN SALAD

Any great salad has a balance of varying textures and flavors. Here, crunchy apples and sharp cheddar cheese complement each other, and the sweet and tangy balsamic dressing is a real crowd-pleaser. Store-bought grilled chicken makes for a healthy meal in a flash.

SERVES 4 TO 6

PREP TIME
10 minutes

INGREDIENTS

FOR THE VINAIGRETTE
(Makes 1 cup)

- ½ cup avocado oil or other neutral oil, such as canola or vegetable
- ¼ cup balsamic vinegar
- 2 tablespoons red wine vinegar
- 1 tablespoon whole grain Dijon mustard
- 1 tablespoon granulated sugar
- ½ teaspoon kosher salt
- ¼ teaspoon garlic powder
- ¼ teaspoon freshly ground black pepper

FOR THE SALAD

- 5 ounces spring lettuce mix
- 1 heart romaine lettuce, chopped
- 2 apples (fuji, gala, or honeycrisp), thinly sliced
- 12 to 16 ounces grilled chicken breast strips, cut into bite-size pieces
- 6 ounces sharp cheddar cheese, cut into ½-inch cubes or coarsely grated
- 1 cup slivered almonds or coarsely chopped walnut or pecan halves

DIRECTIONS

1. Make the vinaigrette: Add the avocado oil, balsamic vinegar, red wine vinegar, mustard, sugar, salt, garlic powder, and pepper to a pint-size jar. Cover and shake to combine. Set aside.

2. Make the salad: Add the lettuce mix, romaine, apples, chicken, cheddar cheese, and almonds to a large salad bowl. Add half the vinaigrette and toss the salad. Try a lettuce leaf to determine whether you'd like to add more vinaigrette. Add more as needed.

3. Transfer the salad to serving bowls and serve right away.

CLYDEO'S TIPS AND TRICKS

Other yummy additions to this salad could be dried cranberries, sliced avocado, chopped celery, thinly sliced red or green onion, or croutons. Any leftover vinaigrette can be stored in a lidded container in the fridge for up to 1 week.

LUNCH

THAI-INSPIRED PEANUT NOODLE SALAD

Peanut dressing flavors a bowl of noodles and crunchy vegetables. Add your protein of choice to make it a main dish. The dressing includes an optional spoonful of sambal oelek, a red pepper paste, for a kick of spice.

SERVES 4

PREP TIME
15 minutes

INGREDIENTS

- 8 ounces pad thai rice noodles (Annie Chun's or Lotus Foods brand)

FOR THE DRESSING

- 2 tablespoons soy sauce
- 2 tablespoons rice vinegar
- 1 tablespoon granulated sugar
- 1 ½ teaspoons sambal oelek chili paste (optional)
- 1 teaspoon sesame oil
- ¼ cup natural peanut butter

FOR THE SALAD

- 1 large carrot, grated
- 1 red bell pepper, julienned
- 4 green onions, sliced thinly

FOR SERVING

- ¼ cup chopped roasted peanuts
- 1 tablespoon chopped fresh cilantro (optional)

DIRECTIONS

1. Place the noodles in a large bowl and cover with hot water. Let the noodles soak for 10 minutes.

2. Make the dressing: While the noodles are soaking, in a small bowl, whisk together the soy sauce, vinegar, sugar, chili paste (if using), oil, and peanut butter until thoroughly combined.

3. Drain the noodles in a colander under cold running water, then transfer them to a large mixing bowl. Add the carrot, bell pepper, green onions, and dressing, and stir until the dressing evenly coats the noodles and vegetables.

4. Transfer the salad to serving bowls. Top with the chopped peanuts and cilantro and serve right away, or store in an airtight container in the fridge for up to 3 days.

CLYDEO'S TIPS AND TRICKS

To turn this salad into a filling entrée, add your favorite protein: store-bought grilled chicken strips, cooked shrimp, or a seared portion of salmon, steak, or tofu.

LUNCH

CHICKEN CAESAR PASTA SALAD

Rotini pasta turns this Caesar salad into a one-bowl meal. Crunchy romaine lettuce and croutons, creamy dressing, and pasta . . . what's not to like? I make this recipe for a hearty lunch on a hot day. It also stores well in the fridge to have on hand as a dinner side dish.

SERVES 4

PREP TIME
10 minutes

INGREDIENTS

FOR THE DRESSING
(Makes about 1 ½ cups)

- 1 cup mayonnaise
- 2 cloves garlic, pressed or grated on a microplane
- 3 tablespoons fresh lemon juice
- 1 tablespoon Dijon mustard
- 1 teaspoon Worcestershire sauce
- ½ cup grated Parmesan cheese
- ¼ teaspoon freshly ground black pepper

FOR THE SALAD

- 2 hearts romaine lettuce, chopped
- 12 to 16 ounces grilled chicken breast strips, cut into bite-size pieces
- ½ pound rotini or other short pasta, cooked and drained
- 2 cups croutons
- ¼ cup grated Parmesan cheese
- Freshly ground black pepper

DIRECTIONS

1 Make the dressing: In a small mixing bowl, whisk together the mayonnaise, garlic, lemon juice, mustard, Worcestershire sauce, Parmesan, and pepper.

2 Make the salad: In a large salad bowl, combine the lettuce, chicken, and pasta. Add ¾ cup of the dressing and toss to combine until all the lettuce leaves are evenly coated in the dressing. Taste a leaf and add more dressing if needed.

3 Transfer the salad to serving plates. Top each salad with croutons, Parmesan, and a few grinds of black pepper. Serve right away, or store in an airtight container in the fridge for up to 3 days.

CLYDEO'S TIPS AND TRICKS

Use any leftover dressing as a dip for carrots and celery. It will keep, refrigerated, for up to 1 week.

39   LUNCH

CHEESY & BEEFY PASTA

Home cooking is so much better than a store-bought box, so I decided to make my very own dish of cheesy, beefy pasta from scratch. It's a savory, meaty, and filling mix of ground beef, macaroni, and peas with a cheddar cheese-y sauce. This is just the kind of dinner hungry kids love.

SERVES 4 TO 6

COOK TIME
25 minutes

INGREDIENTS

- 1 tablespoon olive oil
- 2 cloves garlic, chopped
- 1 medium yellow onion, chopped
- 1 pound ground beef (90% lean or leaner)
- 2 tablespoons tomato paste
- 1 teaspoon Worcestershire sauce
- ½ teaspoon freshly ground black pepper
- 3 cups vegetable broth
- 8 ounces elbow macaroni
- 1 ½ cups shredded cheddar cheese
- 1 cup frozen peas, thawed

FOR SERVING

- 1 tablespoon chopped chives or flat-leaf parsley

41 LUNCH

42

CHEESY & BEEFY PASTA

DIRECTIONS

1 Heat the olive oil and garlic in a 4-quart soup pot over medium heat until the garlic is dancing in the oil. Add the onion and sauté for about 3 minutes, or until it begins to soften. Add the ground beef and sauté for about 5 minutes, or until no pink remains, breaking up the meat with a wooden spoon as it cooks. Stir in the tomato paste, Worcestershire sauce, and pepper.

2 Add the broth and macaroni and stir to combine. Bring to a simmer, then cover the pot and turn the heat down to medium-low. Let simmer for 12 to 15 minutes, stirring occasionally, or until the pasta is tender and cooked through.

3 Turn off the heat. Open the pot and add the cheese and peas. Stir for a minute or so, until the cheese has melted and the peas have warmed through.

4 Spoon into bowls, sprinkle with chives, and serve right away.

> **NOTE** If you don't like vegetable "surprises," leave the peas out or serve them on the side.

LUNCH

THE COZIEST CHICKEN & TORTELLINI SOUP

A cozy and comforting soup filled with cheesy tortellini. Kids can top their own bowls with cheese, parsley, pepper, and a drizzle of olive oil. I love to curl up with a bowl of this soup on a cool day!

SERVES 4 TO 6

PREP TIME
5 minutes

COOK TIME
20 minutes

INGREDIENTS

- 1 tablespoon olive oil
- 1 clove garlic, chopped
- 2 carrots, chopped
- 2 celery stalks, chopped
- 1 small yellow onion, chopped
- ½ teaspoon kosher salt
- ½ teaspoon Italian seasoning
- 4 cups chicken broth
- 1 (14.5-ounce) can petite diced tomatoes
- 1 (10-ounce) package fresh cheese tortellini
- 2 cups (about 10 ounces) shredded cooked rotisserie chicken breast

FOR SERVING

- 4 tablespoons grated Parmesan cheese
- 1 tablespoon chopped fresh flat-leaf parsley
- Freshly ground black pepper
- Olive oil

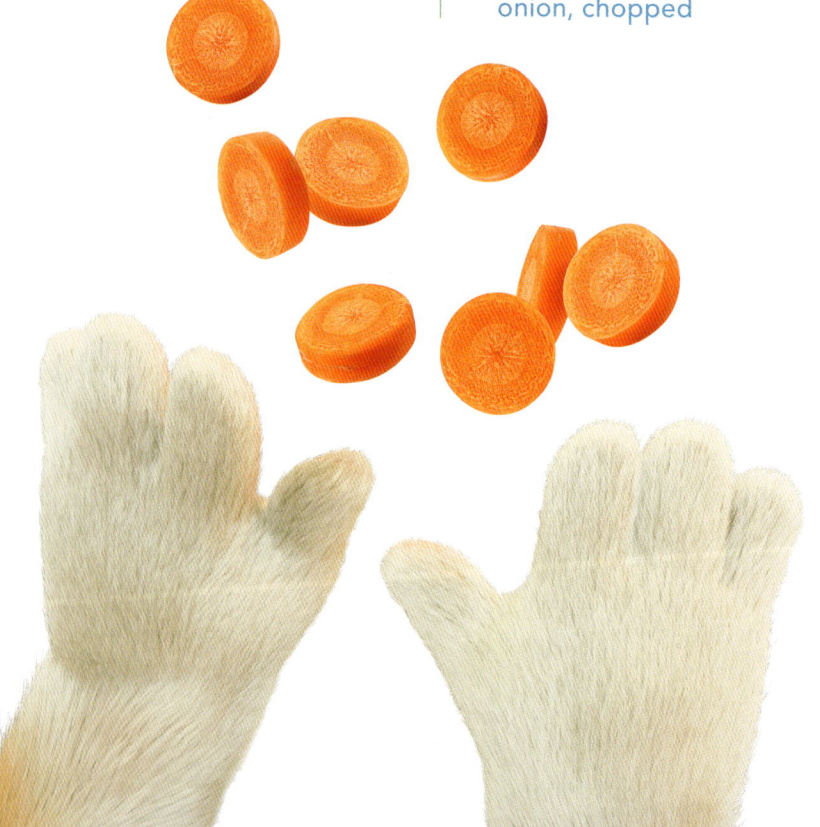

45 LUNCH

"You can serve some garlic bread alongside—it's great for dipping in the broth."

THE COZIEST CHICKEN & TORTELLINI SOUP

DIRECTIONS

1 In a soup pot, heat the olive oil and garlic over medium heat until the garlic is dancing in the oil. Add the carrots, celery, and onion. Sauté for about 5 minutes, or until the onion begins to soften and become translucent.

2 Add the salt, Italian seasoning, broth, tomatoes, tortellini, and chicken breast. Cover and bring to a simmer (this will take around 8 minutes), then turn the heat down to medium-low and let simmer for about 5 minutes, stirring occasionally, or until the tortellini are tender and cooked through. Turn off the heat. Taste the broth for seasoning, adding more salt if needed.

3 Ladle the soup into serving bowls. Top each bowl with Parmesan, parsley, a few grinds of black pepper, and a drizzle of olive oil. Serve right away.

NOTE To add even more veggies to this soup, wilt in a few cups of baby spinach or baby kale right at the end of cooking.

DIY PIZZA BAR

Pizza night is a kid favorite, and mine, too—it's so fun to shape the dough, spread out the sauce, and add toppings to make your custom pie. Make the easy dough recipe in a stand mixer, or use store-bought dough to speed things up.

MAKES 4 PERSONAL PIZZAS

PREP TIME
1 hour

COOK TIME
10 minutes

INGREDIENTS

- 1 pound store-bought pizza dough or

FOR THE PIZZA DOUGH, IF MAKING FRESH

- 2 cups all-purpose flour, plus more for dusting
- 1 teaspoon instant yeast
- 1 teaspoon kosher salt
- ¾ cup warm water (110 to 115°F)

TOPPING SUGGESTIONS

- Marinara sauce or pesto
- Shredded mozzarella cheese
- Sliced pepperoni
- Cooked and crumbled Italian sausage
- Sliced ham
- Sliced bell peppers
- Sliced onions
- Sliced olives
- Pineapple bits

49 LUNCH

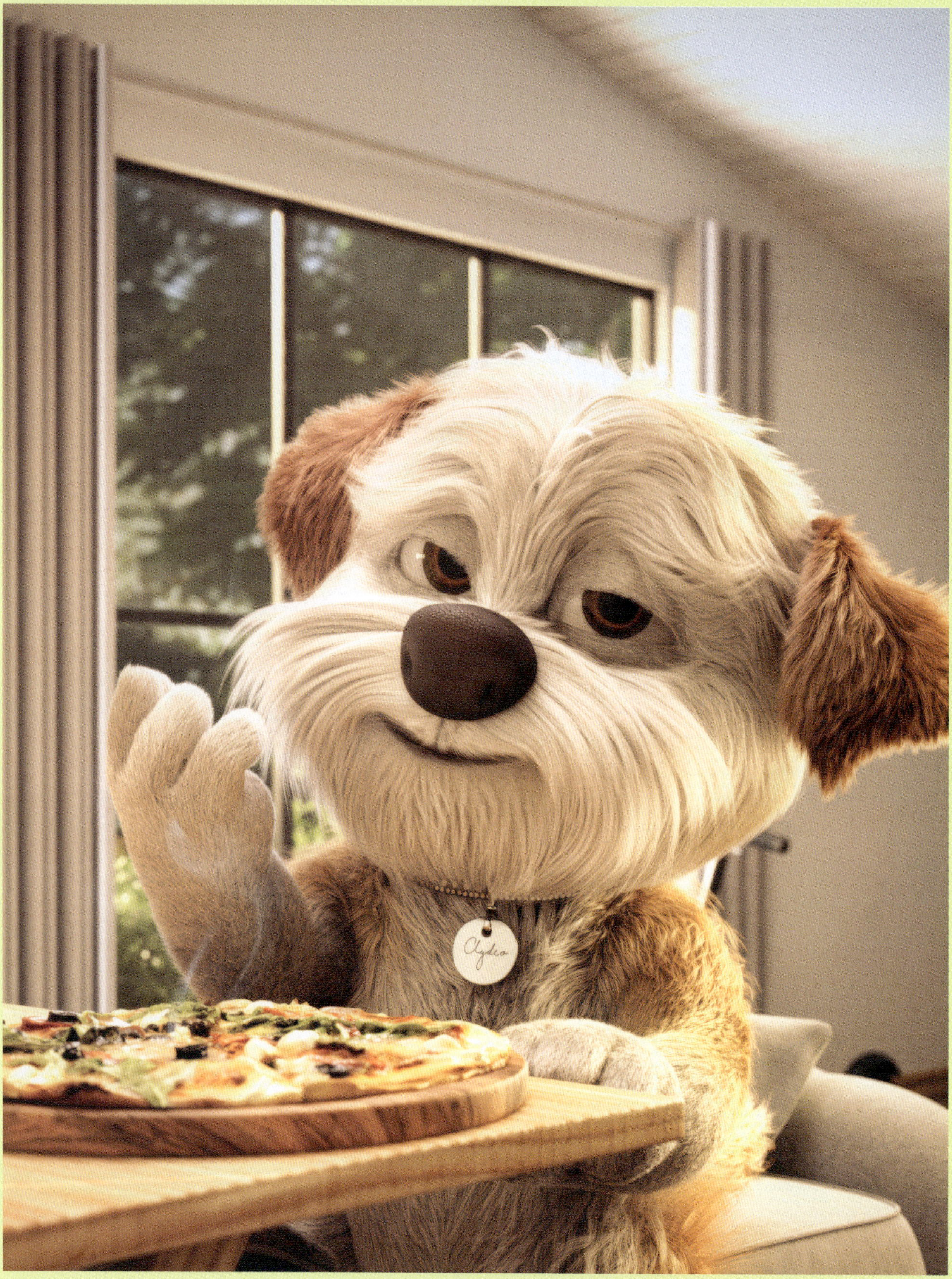
Clydeo

DIY PIZZA BAR

DIRECTIONS

1. If using store-bought dough: Remove it from the refrigerator and let it sit at room temperature for 30 minutes.

2. If making homemade dough: In a stand mixer bowl, combine the flour, yeast, and salt. Stir to combine.

3. Place the bowl in the stand mixer with a dough hook attachment. Add the water, then knead on low speed for about 8 minutes, or until the dough is smooth and elastic.

4. Remove the dough hook, scraping off any dough into the bowl. Cover the bowl with plastic wrap or a reusable lid, and let the dough proof in a warm spot in the kitchen until it has doubled in size, about 40 minutes.

5. Preheat the oven to 425°F with an oven rack in the middle position, on the convection setting if it has one. Line two baking sheets with parchment paper.

6. Transfer the dough to a well-floured work surface and divide the dough into four pieces. Then, using a rolling pin, shape each piece into an 8-inch round, using more flour as needed to prevent the dough from sticking to the surface. Place the rounds of dough onto the prepared baking sheets.

7. Spread each round of dough with marinara or pesto, sprinkle on your mozzarella, then add whatever toppings you like.

8. Bake the pizzas for 10 to 12 minutes, or until the cheese is bubbling and the dough is golden brown around the edges and on the bottom. For even browning, swap the positions of the baking sheets in the oven halfway through cooking.

NOTE: The oven is my favorite warm spot for letting the dough rise. I put it on the "preheat" setting for one minute, then turn it off and place the bowl of dough in the oven. Just remember not to preheat it again until you've taken out the bowl of dough!

LUNCH

DINNER

Ah, dinner. It's a special meal for the Clydes. We all have so much filling up our days—painting, skateboarding, digging, surfing—that it's important for us to sit together, unwind, and share some wonderful food. With how busy everyone is, it can seem overwhelming to make a full dinner, but as Papa Clydely wisely said, "One cannot live on takeout alone." I've cooked up these dishes so that they're easy enough to prepare on even the busiest of nights. Tasty Turkey Meatball Subs (page 58) and Chicken & Vegetable Fried Rice (page 70) can be ready in a flash, but even the "fancier" recipes like my Legendary Lasagna (page 54) and Handmade Sweet Potato Gnocchi (page 66) are weeknight friendly, plus they taste good enough to make anyone sit up and beg for seconds.

53 DINNER

CLYDEO'S LEGENDARY LASAGNA

My favorite dinner! Layers of marinara sauce, noodles, and lots of cheese make an easy and delicious meal. Best of all, the noodles cook in the oven, so it's a single-dish affair, with no extra pots and pans to wash.

CLYDEO'S TIPS AND TRICKS

When I was in Italy, I learned about *la scarpetta*—it means to use a piece of bread to mop up all that delicious leftover sauce that's on your plate. This lasagna is a perfect opportunity to embrace la dolce vita!

SERVES 4 TO 6

PREP TIME
10 minutes
(plus 15 minutes to cool)

COOK TIME
1 hour

INGREDIENTS

- 1 (24-ounce) jar marinara sauce
- 1 box lasagna noodles (you won't need them all)
- 1 (15-ounce) container ricotta cheese
- 2 packed cups (8 ounces) shredded Italian cheese blend
- ½ teaspoon Italian seasoning

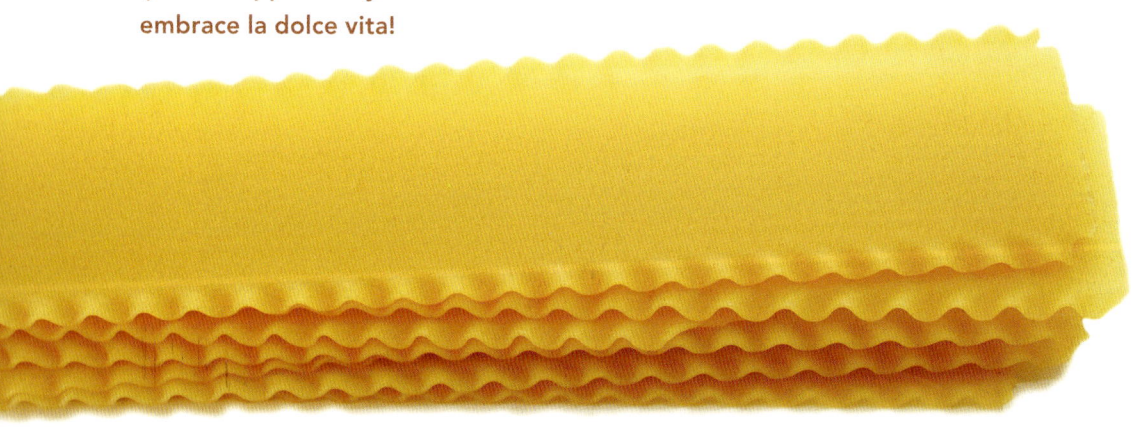

DINNER

I love to use the De Cecco brand "Lasagne no. 1" noodles—they fit perfectly in an 8-inch-square baking dish, two noodles to a layer.

CLYDEO'S LEGENDARY LASAGNA

DIRECTIONS

1 Preheat the oven to 350°F with an oven rack in the middle position.

2 Spoon one-third of the marinara sauce (about 1 cup) into a deep, 8-inch square baking dish and spread it out evenly. Add a single layer of lasagna noodles over the sauce, breaking them to fit if necessary.

3 Spoon half the ricotta cheese on top of the noodles in small dollops, dotting it all over the noodles. Sprinkle on ⅔ cup of the Italian cheese blend, then sprinkle on ¼ teaspoon of the Italian seasoning.

4 Add a second layer of lasagna noodles. Spread out another third of the marinara sauce over the noodles, making sure to cover any dry spots. Dollop on the remaining ricotta, and another ⅔ cup of the Italian cheese blend. Sprinkle on the remaining Italian seasoning.

5 Add a third layer of lasagna noodles. Top with the remaining marinara sauce, again making sure to cover any dry spots of noodle. Sprinkle on the remaining Italian cheese blend, then cover the dish tightly with aluminum foil.

6 Bake the lasagna for 45 minutes, remove the foil, then bake it for about another 15 minutes, or until the cheese on top is bubbly and brown.

7 Remove the lasagna from the oven. Let it cool for at least 15 minutes, then cut into slices and serve hot.

NOTE Add a couple layers of pepperoni or crumbled cooked sausage for meaty lasagna, or blend a few handfuls of baby spinach leaves into the marinara to add some green vegetables.

DINNER

TASTY TURKEY MEATBALL SUBS

I'm crazy for meatballs and sandwiches, so why not have the best of both worlds? Meatballs are piled onto garlic-seasoned hoagie rolls, then topped with savory marinara sauce and melty provolone cheese.

CLYDEO'S TIPS AND TRICKS

I'm a big fan of working smarter, not harder. Bake a double batch of the meatballs and freeze half of them for a quick weeknight meal. To freeze, place them in a single layer on a cookie sheet, place in the freezer until frozen solid (about 2 hours), then transfer to a freezer bag. Just reheat them in the air fryer at 375°F for 10 minutes, or in the oven at 400°F for 12–15 minutes, then add to a saucepan with a jar of pasta sauce and heat on the stove until warmed through. Serve with some spaghetti, and you'll be licking your plate clean in no time!

MAKES 4 SUBS

PREP TIME
10 minutes

COOK TIME
15 minutes

INGREDIENTS

FOR THE MEATBALLS

- 1 pound ground turkey (93% lean)
- ½ cup panko breadcrumbs
- 1 large egg
- ½ teaspoon Italian seasoning
- ½ teaspoon kosher salt
- Olive oil or avocado oil spray

FOR THE SUBS

- 4 hoagie sandwich rolls
- 2 tablespoons olive oil
- ½ teaspoon garlic salt
- 1 ⅓ cups marinara sauce
- 1 packed cup (4 ounces) shredded provolone cheese

59 DINNER

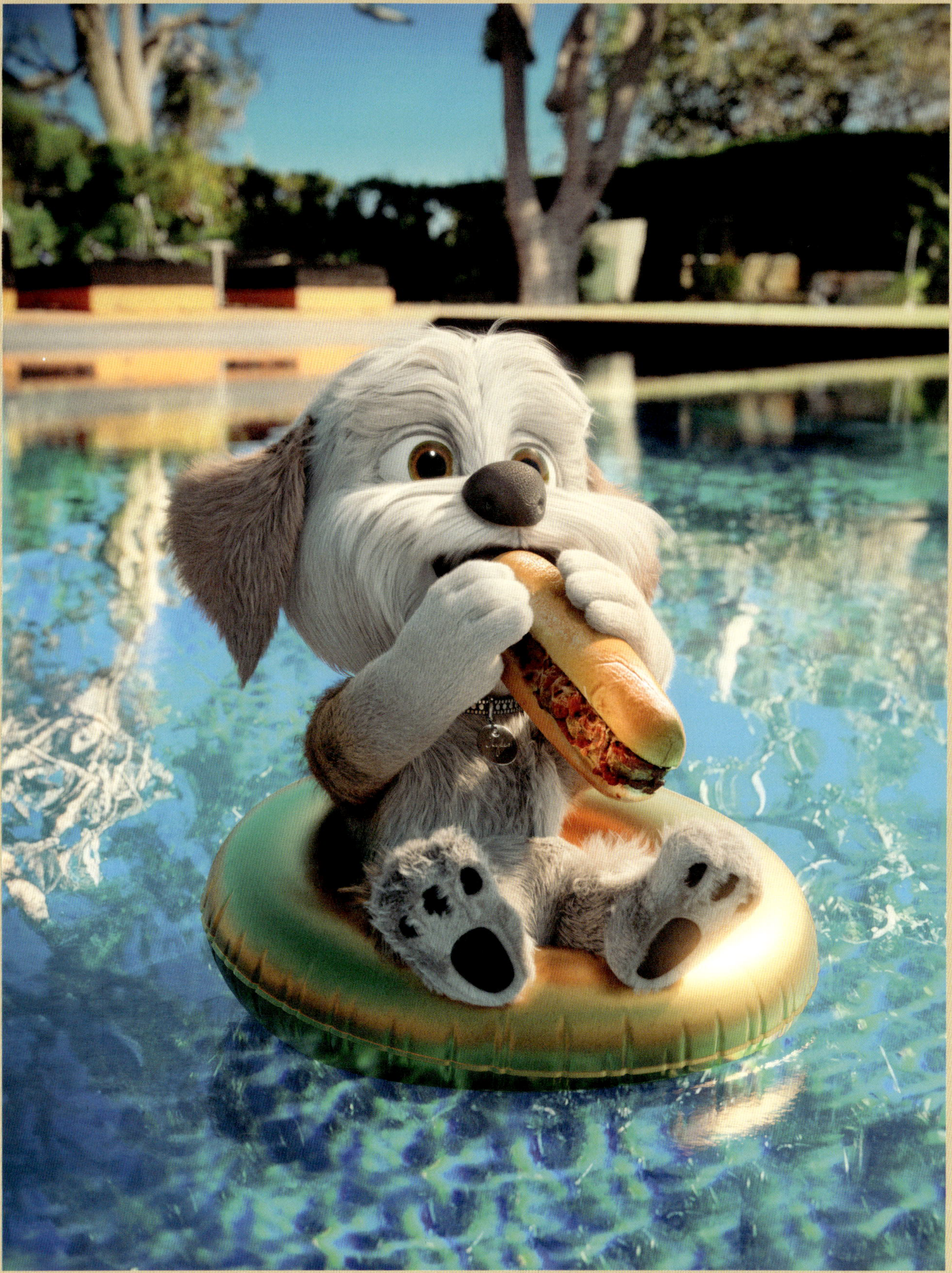

TASTY TURKEY MEATBALL SUBS

DIRECTIONS

1 Preheat the oven to 400°F. Line two baking sheets with parchment paper.

2 Make the meatballs: In a large mixing bowl, stir together the turkey, breadcrumbs, egg, Italian seasoning, and salt until evenly combined. Use a 1 ½-tablespoon cookie scoop to portion out the meatballs onto one of the prepared baking sheets. You should have about 16 meatballs. Spray the meatballs lightly with olive oil.

3 Bake the meatballs for 10 to 12 minutes, or until cooked through and lightly brown on the bottoms.

4 Make the subs: While the meatballs are baking, place the hoagie rolls on the other prepared baking sheet. Split open the rolls, drizzle their insides with the olive oil, then sprinkle with the garlic salt.

5 Remove the meatballs from the oven, place four meatballs on each of the bottom rolls, spoon the marinara sauce over the meatballs, and sprinkle the cheese on the tops of the rolls.

6 Bake the subs for about 5 minutes, or until the bread is toasted and the cheese is melty. Remove from the oven, transfer to serving plates, and serve right away.

Simplify this recipe with store-bought meatballs, if you like! They can be found in the freezer section of most grocery stores.

DINNER

TACO 'BOUT A GOOD BURGER

I love the smell of these sizzling hamburger tacos, and you will, too! Set up a bar of burger toppings so everybody can top these how they like. Smashed onto flour tortillas, the burgers cook quickly. These kid-size tacos are gone in a flash.

MAKES 8 BURGER TACOS

PREP TIME
10 minutes

COOK TIME
10 minutes

INGREDIENTS

FOR THE SAUCE

- ½ cup mayonnaise
- 2 tablespoons ketchup
- 2 tablespoons yellow mustard
- 2 tablespoons dill pickle relish
- ¼ teaspoon freshly ground black pepper
- ¼ teaspoon garlic powder
- ¼ teaspoon onion powder

FOR THE BURGERS

- 1 pound ground beef (90% lean or leaner)
- 8 small (street taco–size) flour tortillas
- Kosher salt and freshly ground black pepper or burger seasoning (see page 64)
- Cooking oil spray, such as canola or vegetable oil
- 8 slices American or cheddar cheese

TOPPINGS

- ½ small head iceberg lettuce, shredded
- 2 tomatoes, diced
- ½ small yellow onion, diced
- 24 dill pickle slices
- Ketchup
- Mustard
- Salt and pepper, to taste

63 DINNER

Burger seasoning takes these to another level. Either buy a spice blend at the store or mix together: 1 tablespoon kosher salt, 2 teaspoons freshly ground black pepper, 2 teaspoons garlic powder, 1 teaspoon onion powder, 1 teaspoon sugar, 1 teaspoon paprika, and 1/2 teaspoon ground cumin. Makes about 1/4 cup. Use around 1/4 teaspoon per burger in step 2.

TACO 'BOUT A GOOD BURGER

DIRECTIONS

1 Make the sauce: In a small mixing bowl, stir together the mayonnaise, ketchup, mustard, pickle relish, pepper, garlic powder, and onion powder until thoroughly combined. Set aside.

2 Make the burgers: Divide the ground beef into eight equal pieces. Use your fingers to evenly spread out each piece of ground beef onto a tortilla, all the way to the edges. Sprinkle a little salt and pepper evenly over each burger.

3 Heat a griddle or large skillet over medium heat. Spray with of cooking oil, then add the smash burgers to the griddle, meat side down. (Add as many as will fit without overlapping; you may need to cook in batches.) Let them cook for about 3 minutes, or until the burgers are browned and cooked through. Flip the burgers onto their tortilla side, top each burger with a slice of American cheese, and let cook for 1 more minute or so, to crisp the tortillas and allow the cheese to melt a little.

4 Transfer the burgers to plates. Serve them right away, with the burger sauce and toppings alongside.

NOTE For an easy side dish, heat up a bag of store-bought fries or Tater Tots.

HANDMADE SWEET POTATO GNOCCHI

There's nothing better than a hearty pasta dish. Sweet potatoes give these tender gnocchi their beautiful orange color. I love to cook with my family and friends, and making these handmade sweet potato gnocchi is a fun activity everyone can enjoy!

MAKES ABOUT 4 DOZEN GNOCCHI

PREP TIME
20 minutes

COOK TIME
10 minutes

INGREDIENTS

- 2 medium (8-ounce) sweet potatoes
- 1 large egg yolk
- ¼ teaspoon plus 2 tablespoons kosher salt, divided
- 1 cup all-purpose flour, plus more as needed
- 2 tablespoons unsalted butter
- 2 tablespoons olive oil
- Freshly ground black pepper
- Grated Parmesan cheese

> This recipe works with other potatoes, too. The amount of flour you'll need will depend on how much moisture is in them. Try yukon gold, russet, or purple potatoes.

67 DINNER

CLYDEO'S TIPS AND TRICKS

If you like, you can roast your sweet potatoes in an air fryer instead of cooking them in the microwave. Roast at 375°F for 25 minutes, then check for doneness.

HANDMADE SWEET POTATO GNOCCHI

DIRECTIONS

1. Heat 3 quarts of water in a large pot over medium heat. While the water is coming to a boil, make the gnocchi.

2. Prick the sweet potatoes all over with a fork and place them in a microwave-safe dish. Microwave for 5 minutes. Check for doneness—you should be able to easily insert a paring knife into the thickest part of the sweet potato. If they're not done, microwave for another couple of minutes, until they're soft all the way through.

3. Let the sweet potatoes cool down for a few minutes, until you can comfortably peel off their skins. Discard the skins and place the sweet potatoes in a medium mixing bowl. Using a fork or potato masher, mash them, making sure there are no lumps left behind.

4. Add the egg yolk and the ¼ teaspoon of salt, and mix until thoroughly combined. Add the flour. Using a spoon or dough whisk, bring the mixture together into a cohesive ball of dough. If it's very sticky, add a bit more flour.

5. Flour a work surface. Transfer your dough to the work surface, then knead it gently for 1 to 2 minutes, adding more flour if needed, or until the dough is workable and no longer sticky.

6. Divide the dough into two pieces. Roll each piece into a long snake, about 1 inch in diameter.

7. Using a butter knife or bench scraper, cut the snakes of dough into bite-size pillows. Use a gnocchi board or a fork to add a ridged pattern to the gnocchi, if you like.

8. When the water begins to boil, add the 2 tablespoons of salt, then add half the gnocchi.

9. Place a large skillet on the stove over medium heat. Add 1 tablespoon each of the butter and olive oil.

10. When the gnocchi are cooked, after a minute or two, they will float to the surface of the water. Use a slotted spoon or spider strainer to transfer the gnocchi to the skillet. Sauté for 3 to 4 minutes, or until the gnocchi are lightly browned. Transfer the gnocchi to serving plates, covering with aluminum foil to keep them warm.

11. Cook and sauté the remaining gnocchi.

12. Top the gnocchi with a few grinds of black pepper and a sprinkle of Parmesan. Serve right away.

CHICKEN & VEGETABLE FRIED RICE

A leftovers makeover never tasted so good. With a little soy sauce, some eggs, thawed frozen veggies, and a sprinkle of green onions, cooked rice and rotisserie chicken breast turn into a delicious one-pan dinner.

SERVES 4

COOK TIME
15 minutes

INGREDIENTS

- 2 tablespoons avocado oil or other neutral oil, such as canola or vegetable, divided
- 4 eggs, whisked
- 2 cloves garlic, finely chopped
- 3 cups cooked rice (from 1 cup uncooked rice)
- 2 cups frozen mixed vegetables, thawed
- 2 cups diced cooked chicken breast
- 2 tablespoons soy sauce
- 2 green onions, thinly sliced
- Kosher salt

DINNER

72

CHICKEN & VEGETABLE FRIED RICE

DIRECTIONS

1 Heat 1 tablespoon of the avocado oil in a large pan or high-sided skillet over medium heat. Add the eggs and scramble until they're cooked but still a bit shiny—you don't want them to get too dry. Transfer the eggs to a dish and return the pan to the stove.

2 Add the remaining oil to the pan, along with the garlic. When the garlic begins to dance in the oil, add the rice. Sauté the rice for about 3 minutes, or until it is warmed through and the grains are separate and fluffy. Add the vegetables and chicken and stir to combine them evenly with the rice.

3 Drizzle in the soy sauce and mix together for 2 minutes. Add the cooked eggs and sauté for 1 more minute, breaking up the eggs with a spatula and tossing them in with the rest of the ingredients.

4 Turn off the heat. Sprinkle in the green onions and toss to combine. Taste for seasoning, adding salt if needed.

5 Transfer the fried rice to serving dishes and serve right away.

NOTE Switch up the vegetables and protein in the fried rice based on what you have lying around. Try subbing in chopped cooked broccoli or green beans for the mixed vegetables, and Chinese sausage or shrimp for the chicken.

LOADED HOT DOG BAR

How do you like your hot dogs? Topped with chili and cheese, "dragged through the garden" with pickled vegetables, piled with tangy sauerkraut and mustard, or with a zigzag of ketchup? With a hot dog bar, everyone can choose their favorite style. Serve fries or tots on the side.

MAKES 8 HOT DOGS

PREP TIME
15 minutes

COOK TIME
5 minutes

INGREDIENTS
- 8 hot dogs (whatever variety you like)
- 8 hot dog buns (regular, brioche, or pretzel), warmed

TOPPINGS
- Yellow mustard
- Ketchup
- Chopped onions
- Sauerkraut
- Chili, warmed
- Shredded cheddar cheese
- Giardiniera (pickled vegetables)
- Pickle relish
- Celery salt

DIRECTIONS

1. Bring a pot of water to boil over medium heat. Add the hot dogs and boil for 5 minutes, then turn off the heat.

2. Place the hot dog buns on serving plates, then, using tongs, transfer the hot dogs to the buns.

3. Let everyone top their hot dogs as they like with any of the toppings.

NOTE: The selection of toppings here includes the basic ingredients for hot dogs (ketchup and/or mustard, and onions or sauerkraut if you like), chili dogs, and Chicago-inspired hot dogs.

CLYDEO'S TIPS AND TRICKS

If you prefer, you can grill, pan-fry, or even air fry your hot dogs. Cook them whole or split them down the middle for more browning.

75 DINNER

POT ROAST FRENCH DIP SANDWICHES

I love to make these decadent French dip sandwiches for a wholesome dinner. The pot roast is cooked low and slow, then sliced or shredded and tucked into sandwich rolls for an easy dinner. Everyone gets a little bowl of the savory cooking liquid (aka jus) to dunk their sandwich in.

MAKES 6 SANDWICHES

PREP TIME
20 minutes

COOK TIME
3 hours

INGREDIENTS

- Beef chuck roast (2 ½ to 3 pounds)
- 1 teaspoon kosher salt
- 1 teaspoon freshly ground black pepper
- 1 tablespoon avocado oil or other neutral oil, such as canola or vegetable
- 1 large yellow onion, sliced
- 4 cloves garlic, minced
- 4 cups low-sodium vegetable broth
- 1 tablespoon Dijon mustard
- 1 tablespoon Worcestershire sauce
- 1 sprig fresh rosemary
- 6 French bread or ciabatta sandwich rolls, toasted

DINNER

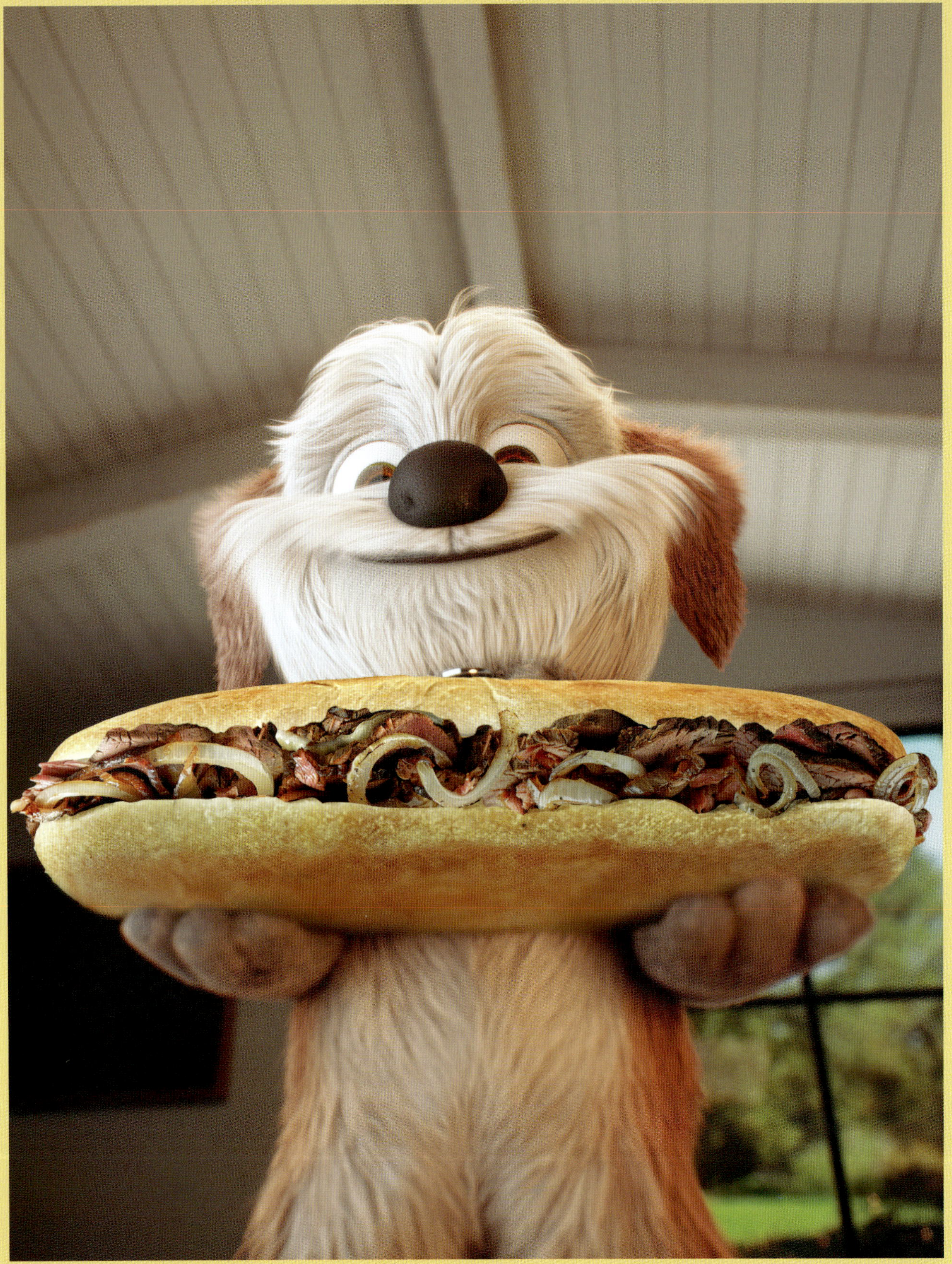

POT ROAST FRENCH DIP SANDWICHES

DIRECTIONS

1. Preheat the oven to 325°F with an oven rack in the middle position.

2. Season the roast all over with the salt and pepper.

3. Heat a Dutch oven on the stovetop over medium heat, then add the avocado oil.

4. Add the roast to the Dutch oven and let it sear for about 5 minutes, or until it easily releases from the pot. Using a pair of tongs, flip it over and sear the other side for another 5 minutes, then transfer to a dish.

5. Add the onion and garlic to the pot and sauté for about 3 minutes, or until the onion begins to soften. Add the broth, mustard, Worcestershire sauce, and rosemary and stir to combine, using a wooden spoon to scrape up any browned bits from the bottom of the pot.

6. Add the pot roast back to the pot. Cover the pot, transfer to the oven, and let roast for 2 ½ hours.

7. Transfer the pot roast to a carving board. Remove the rosemary spring and, using a slotted spoon, transfer the onion to a dish, then strain the cooking liquid through a fat separator or skim the fat off the top with a ladle.

8. Slice the pot roast (or shred it if it is too soft to slice), then tuck it into the sandwich rolls, along with some of the sliced onion. Serve each sandwich with a ramekin of the cooking liquid on the side for dipping.

For a zing of spice, serve cream-style horseradish on the side or spread a little on the sandwich rolls.

DINNER

SNACKS & SIDES

Living with Jen certainly has its perks. Beyond having a well-stocked kitchen, there always seems to be someone around to share my culinary creations with, which is good news, because the fridge is full of hummus from trying to perfect my recipe! While there have been a few lessons learned and messes to clean along the way (make sure the lid is tightly secured on your blender—sorry, Lord Chesterfield!), these are some time-tested recipes that I love to share. Whether you're craving some nibbles to enjoy by the pool or searching for a late-night snack, I've got you covered. Now, who wants some hummus?

81   SNACKS & SIDES

QUESO DIP

Inspired by Tex-Mex cuisine, this quick and easy queso dip is a snack I love to make—and eat! Made-from-scratch queso is hard to beat. My version uses Colby-Jack cheese, grated by hand to ensure an extra-smooth dip.

SERVES 4 TO 6

PREP TIME
5 minutes

COOK TIME
10 minutes

INGREDIENTS

- 8 ounces Colby-Jack cheese
- 1 teaspoon cornstarch
- 2 tablespoons unsalted butter
- 2 tablespoons all-purpose flour
- 1 cup whole milk
- 1 (4-ounce) can diced roasted green peppers
- ¼ teaspoon chili powde
- ¼ teaspoon cumin
- ½ teaspoon kosher salt

FOR SERVING

- Tortilla chips

DIRECTIONS

1. Grate the Colby-Jack cheese. Add it to a large mixing bowl and toss with the cornstarch, making sure all the cheese is coated in a light layer of cornstarch.

2. Melt the butter in a 2-quart saucepan over medium heat. Add the flour and cook for 1 to 2 minutes, stirring often, or until the roux is bubbly, blond in color, and smells a little bit toasty.

3. Pour the milk into the roux in a thin stream, whisking as you go to prevent any lumps. Once you've added all the milk, let the mixture come back to a boil and thicken. Add the diced peppers, chili powder, cumin, and salt. Stir to combine, then turn the heat down to its lowest setting.

4. Add the cheese in handfuls, stirring in each handful as you go and making sure it is all melted in before adding more. Once you've added the last handful of cheese, turn off the heat and stir until smooth.

5. Pour the queso into a serving bowl or mini Crock-Pot on its lowest setting, and serve with tortilla chips for dipping.

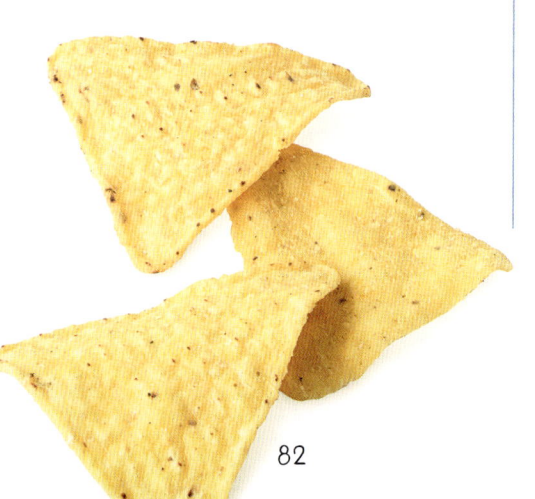

CLYDEO'S TIPS AND TRICKS

Choose either mild or spicy roasted green peppers depending on how much heat you like in your queso. And if you like an all-white queso, substitute Monterey Jack for the Colby-Jack.

VERY BERRY SMOOTHIE

A berry good smoothie! Keep frozen fruit on hand to whip up a smoothie anytime. This one uses bananas and berries for a sweet and beautifully purple sipper.

CLYDEO'S TIPS AND TRICKS

Smoothies are my favorite post-yoga snack! They're also a great way to experiment with different flavor combinations and sneak in some extra veggies. Sometimes I add a handful of spinach or kale when I'm feeling healthy. And the best part is you can't even taste the veggies because of all the delicious fruit.

SERVES 2 TO 3

PREP TIME
5 minutes

INGREDIENTS

- 1 large banana, peeled and broken into chunks
- 1 cup frozen mango or pineapple chunks
- 1 cup frozen blueberries
- 1 cup frozen strawberries
- 2 cups fruit juice (pineapple, mango, or apple juice)

DIRECTIONS

1. In a blender, combine the banana, frozen fruit, and fruit juice. Start the blender at low speed, gradually bring it up to high speed, then blend for about 30 seconds, or until smooth. If the smoothie does not blend easily, add another splash of fruit juice, stir, and blend once more.

2. Pour the smoothie into glasses and serve right away.

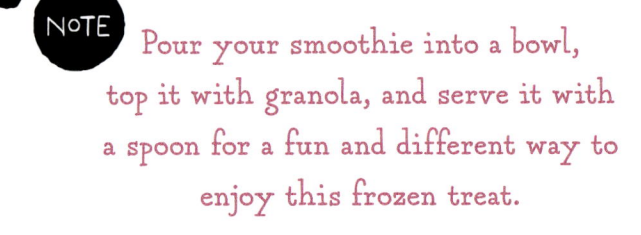

NOTE Pour your smoothie into a bowl, top it with granola, and serve it with a spoon for a fun and different way to enjoy this frozen treat.

85 SNACKS & SIDES

JENNIFER ANISTON'S EASY ENCHILADA BITES

These crispy, one-bite tortilla cups have a cheesy, saucy filling that tastes like your favorite enchilada. A dollop of guac adds a cooling, fresh contrast to the hot and melty cheese.

MAKES 24 BITES

PREP TIME
10 minutes

COOK TIME
20 minutes

INGREDIENTS

- 6 (8-inch) flour tortillas
- 1 tablespoon avocado oil or other neutral oil, such as canola or vegetable
- ½ cup (2 ounces) shredded cheddar cheese
- ½ cup (2 ounces) shredded Monterey Jack cheese
- ¾ cup enchilada sauce
- ½ medium yellow onion, diced
- ½ cup (2 ounces) Cotija cheese, crumbled or grated

FOR SERVING

- Guacamole (store-bought or homemade, see page 89)

87 SNACKS & SIDES

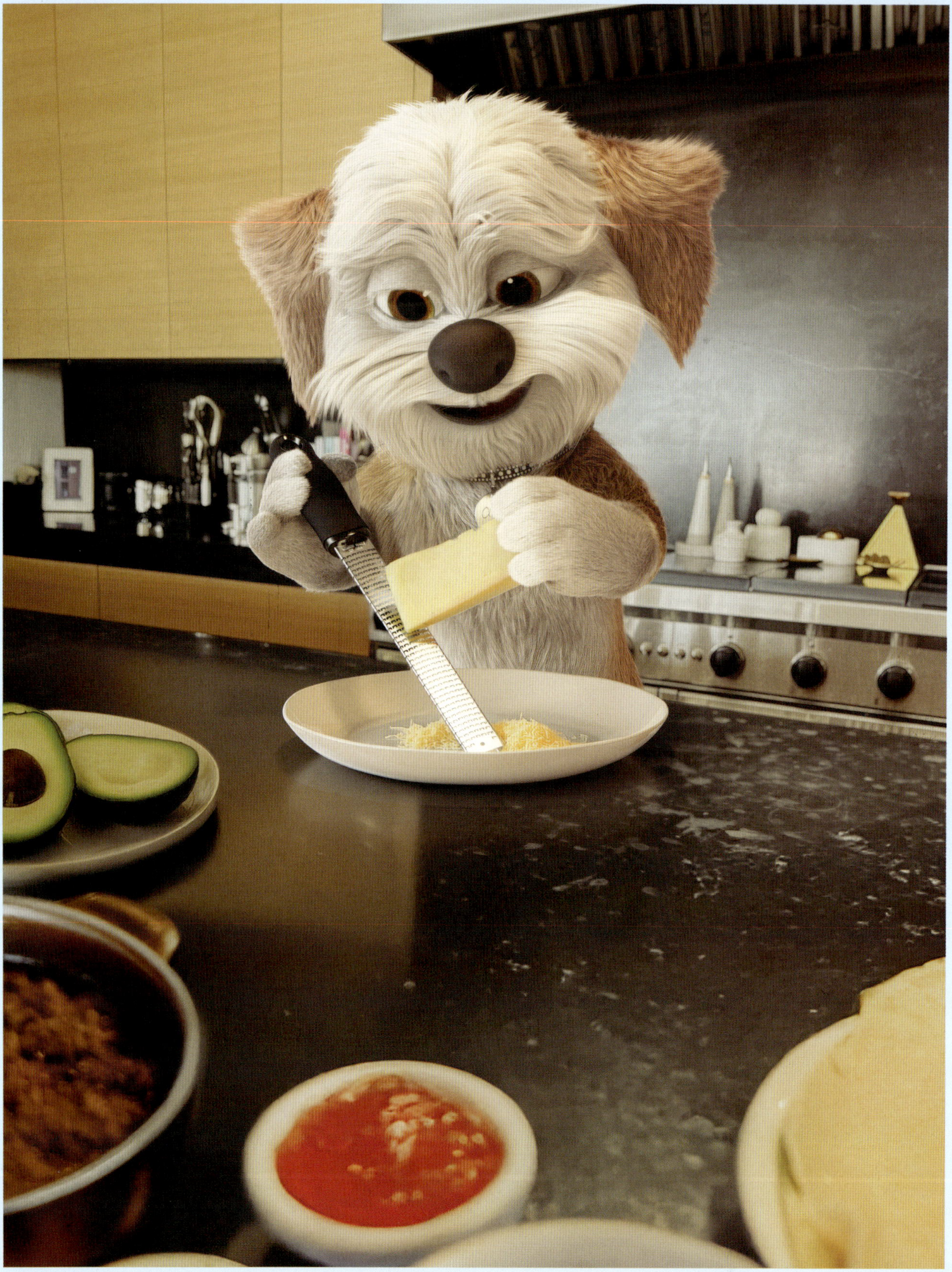

JENNIFER ANISTON'S EASY ENCHILADA BITES

DIRECTIONS

1 Preheat the oven to 350°F with the oven rack in the middle position.

2 Place the tortillas on a cutting board. Using a 2 ½-to-3-inch circular cookie cutter, cut out 24 tortilla rounds (if you don't have a cookie cutter, use a drinking glass or measuring cup).

3 Brush one side of each tortilla round with the avocado oil. Push the tortilla rounds into muffin tins, oiled side down, to make little cups.

4 In a small bowl, mix together the cheddar and Monterey Jack.

5 Into each tortilla cup, spoon about 1 ½ teaspoons of enchilada sauce, 1 ½ teaspoons of diced onion, and 2 teaspoons of the cheese mix.

6 Bake the enchilada bites for 20 to 25 minutes, or until the cheese has melted and the tortillas are crispy and golden on the bottoms.

7 Remove the enchilada bites from the oven and transfer to a serving dish. Sprinkle the crumbled Cotija cheese on top. Serve right away, with guacamole on the side.

> To make a super-simple guacamole, mash up 2 large avocados with 2 tablespoons fresh lime juice, 1 tablespoon chopped cilantro, ¼ cup diced onion, ½ teaspoon garlic powder, and ¼ teaspoon kosher salt, or more to taste.

SNACKS & SIDES

MINI BRUSCHETTA BITES

I am always ready for a crunchy, salty snack! Diced tomatoes are tossed with garlic, spices, vinegar, and olive oil to make a fresh and tasty topping for toasted, crusty bread.

MAKES 24 BITES

PREP TIME
10 minutes

COOK TIME
5 minutes

INGREDIENTS

FOR THE TOPPING

- 3 Roma tomatoes or 12 Campari tomatoes, seeded and diced
- 1 tablespoon extra-virgin olive oil
- 2 teaspoons aged balsamic vinegar
- 1 clove garlic, diced
- ¼ teaspoon Italian seasoning
- ½ teaspoon kosher salt
- ⅛ teaspoon freshly ground black pepper

FOR THE TOAST

- 1 baguette, sliced into ½-inch-thick rounds, 24 total (you may have extra baguette left over)
- 1 large clove garlic, peeled
- 2 tablespoons olive oil

DIRECTIONS

1. Make the topping: In a medium mixing bowl, gently mix together until evenly combined the tomatoes, extra-virgin olive oil, vinegar, garlic, Italian seasoning, salt, and pepper.

2. Make the toast: Toast the baguette slices in a toaster oven on a baking tray for about 5 minutes, or until they're golden brown. (If you don't have a toaster oven, bake in the oven at 425°F for 5 minutes, with the oven rack in the middle position.) When the toast is cool enough to handle, rub each slice with the garlic clove, then drizzle with the olive oil.

3. Place the toast on a serving dish and spoon a little of the topping onto each toast. Serve right away.

NOTE If you have some fresh basil on hand, use a tablespoon, chopped, in place of the Italian seasoning.

91 SNACKS & SIDES

HEALTHY & HEARTY HOMEMADE HUMMUS

Hummus made fresh at home? Absolutely. Canned chickpeas are brought up to a simmer and blended while they're warm for the creamiest, dreamiest dip. Serve it with wedges of pita bread, chips, or veggies.

SERVES 8

PREP TIME
5 minutes

COOK TIME
5 minutes

INGREDIENTS

- 1 (15-ounce) can chickpeas, drained and rinsed
- ⅓ cup tahini
- ¼ cup olive oil, plus more for serving
- ¼ cup water
- 3 tablespoons fresh lemon juice
- 1 clove garlic
- ¾ teaspoon kosher salt
- Paprika, for serving

DIRECTIONS

1. Set aside a couple of tablespoons of the chickpeas for garnish.

2. In a 1-quart saucepan, add the remaining chickpeas and enough water to cover them. Bring the chickpeas to a simmer over medium heat (this will take about 5 minutes). Turn off the heat.

3. Drain the chickpeas in a colander, then place them in a food processor along with the tahini, olive oil, water, lemon juice, garlic, and salt. Process for 2 to 3 minutes or until very smooth, scraping down the sides halfway through processing.

4. Transfer the hummus to a serving dish. Sprinkle the reserved chickpeas on top, then drizzle with olive oil and sprinkle with paprika. Serve right away or store in an airtight container in the fridge for up to 3 days.

CLYDEO'S TIPS AND TRICKS

Add one jar of roasted red peppers for a red pepper hummus.

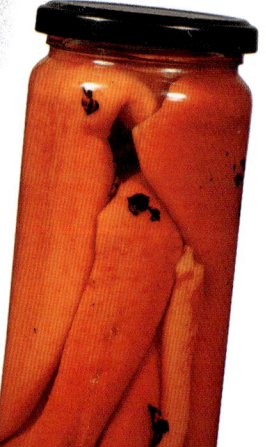

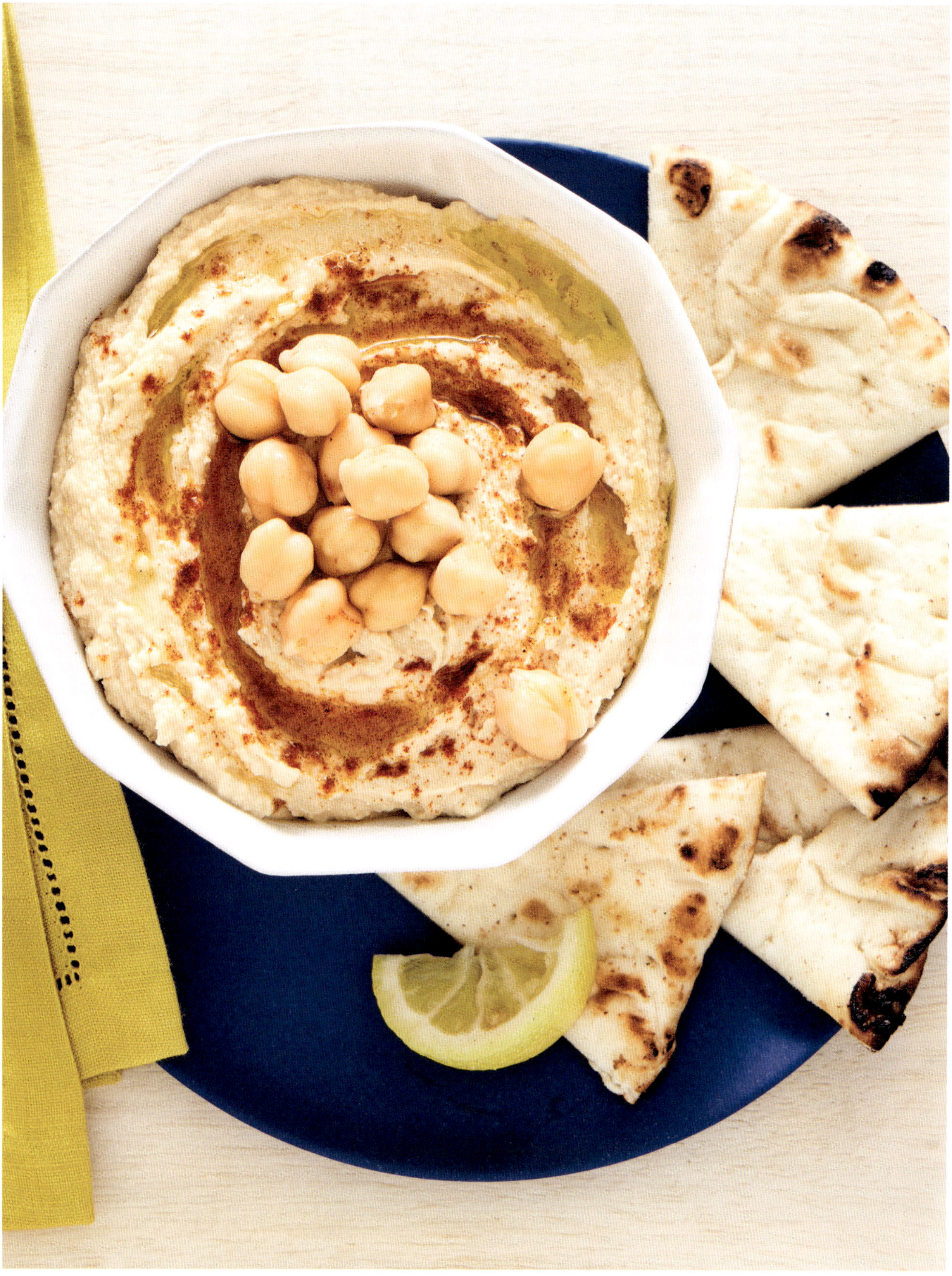

HOW TO BUILD A CHARCUTERIE & CHEESE BOARD

Charcuterie and cheese make the perfect starter for any gathering or even a special treat for a casual night at home. Snack away on this beautiful board filled with your favorite nibbles. It's as fun to put together as it is to eat.

MAKES 1 BOARD

PREP TIME
15 minutes

INGREDIENTS

- 1 semisoft to hard cheese (cheddar, Swiss, smoked or aged Gouda, Muenster, etc.), 3 ounces per person
- 1 soft cheese (brie, goat cheese, Camembert, Boursin, cream cheese, etc.), 3 ounces per person
- 2 cured meats (prosciutto, salami, pepperoni, summer sausage, saucisson, etc.), 2 to 3 slices per person
- Roasted nuts (almonds, cashews, walnuts, pecans, macadamia nuts, etc.)
- Olives or pickles (black or green olives, cornichons, dilly beans, pickled onions, etc.)
- 1 dried fruit (apricots, figs, apple rings, raisins, cranberries, etc.)
- 1 fresh fruit (strawberries, grapes, tangerines, sliced apples or pears, etc.)
- Crackers (wheat, snack, water, saltines, club, etc.)

95 SNACKS & SIDES

For a doggy theme, cut a piece of cardboard into the shape of a dog bone or paw, cover with aluminum foil, and use it as your board. (Just remember, the snacks aren't dog-friendly!)

HOW TO BUILD A CHARCUTERIE & CHEESE BOARD

DIRECTIONS

1 Place the two types of cheeses on opposite ends of a serving board or large dish.

2 Place the cured meats on opposite ends of the board.

3 Place bowls of roasted nuts and olives or pickles on opposite ends of the board.

4 Arrange the dried fruit, fresh fruit, and crackers around the meats, cheeses, and bowls of nuts and pickles, filling in any gaps.

NOTE *If you like, you can add condiments such as whole-grain mustard, jam, or marmalade to your board. Rounds of baguette are a nice addition, too.*

TOAST, BUT MAKE IT PIZZA!

For as long as there have been after-school snacks, there has been pizza toast. Spread a little pizza sauce on any sturdy bread, then sprinkle on cheese and your favorite toppings.

SERVES 4

PREP TIME
10 minutes

COOK TIME
5 minutes

INGREDIENTS

- 4 slices bread (French bread, sourdough, or ciabatta)
- ½ cup pizza sauce
- 1 cup shredded mozzarella cheese
- Your favorite pizza toppings

DIRECTIONS

1. Place the bread on a toaster oven baking sheet.

2. Using a spoon or spatula, spread the pizza sauce on the slices of bread. Sprinkle with the cheese, followed by your favorite pizza toppings.

3. Toast the pizza toast for 5 to 7 minutes, or until the cheese is bubbling and beginning to brown. Let cool for 5 minutes, then serve.

What are your favorite pizza toppings? Pepperoni, bell peppers, onions, olives, or pineapple?

SNACKS & SIDES

SWEET POTATO NACHOS

Bake thin slices of sweet potato to make crispy chips, then layer them with beans, cheese, sour cream, and salsa. Check out my tip for even more fun toppings.

SERVES 4

PREP TIME
10 minutes

COOK TIME
25 minutes

INGREDIENTS

- 1 large (14-to-16-ounce) sweet potato
- Avocado oil spray
- Kosher salt and freshly ground black pepper
- 1 cup cooked black beans
- 1 cup (4 ounces) grated Monterey Jack or Colby-Jack cheese

FOR SERVING

- ¼ cup sour cream
- ¼ cup salsa
- 1 tablespoon chopped cilantro (optional)

DIRECTIONS

1. Preheat the oven to 350°F with the oven rack in the middle position. Line two baking sheets with parchment paper or aluminum foil.

2. Using a mandolin or a chef's knife, cut the sweet potato into very thin slices (⅛ inch or thinner).

3. Place the sweet potato slices on the prepared baking sheets in a single layer. Spray the slices with avocado oil and sprinkle them lightly with salt and pepper. Turn the slices over, and repeat.

4. Bake the slices for 15 minutes, flip them, and bake for 5 minutes more. Remove from the oven.

5. Sprinkle ½ cup each of the black beans and cheese evenly over one baking sheet of chips. Top with the chips from the second baking sheet, and sprinkle on the remaining black beans and cheese. Bake for about 5 minutes, or until the cheese has melted.

6. Transfer the nachos to a big serving plate. Dollop on sour cream and salsa, sprinkle on cilantro, and serve right away.

CLYDEO'S TIPS AND TRICKS

Want to go even more deluxe? Load your nachos up with seasoned taco beef, queso (see page 82), chopped onions, cubed avocado, or a sprinkle of Cotija cheese.

101 SNACKS & SIDES

DESSERTS & DOG TREAT

Cookies and milk, donuts and coffee, cupcakes and . . . anything; these are a few of my favorite sweet pairings. These recipes are great for sharing with your pack or, let's be honest, enjoying all by yourself. Dogs can't share any chocolate creations, so I've got some special 4-Ingredient Homemade Dog Treats (page 118) just for my doggie friends—and yours! They smell so yummy, you may be tempted to take a nibble yourself. Grab some dessert, cuddle up on the couch, and enjoy a sweet ending to another day.

103 DESSERTS & DOG TREAT

NO-BAKE OREO PIE

Sometimes I'm not up for baking, so I put together this no-bake dessert. See if you can dunk the cookies in milk and arrange them in the pie pan without eating at least one!

SERVES 6 TO 8

PREP TIME
15 minutes
(plus 6 hours to chill)

INGREDIENTS

- 1 (18-ounce) family-size package Oreo sandwich cookies
- 1 cup whole milk
- 2 (8-ounce) tubs Cool Whip
- ¼ cup mini chocolate chips

DIRECTIONS

1. Dunk an Oreo cookie in the milk for a few seconds, then place it in a pie pan. Continue dunking and adding cookies to the pie pan until you have a single layer all along the bottom and sides of the pan.

2. Add 1 tub of the Cool Whip to the pan and spread it evenly over the cookies. Dunk and place another layer of cookies on top of the Cool Whip.

3. Top the pie with the remaining tub of Cool Whip, then sprinkle the mini chocolate chips evenly over the top.

4. Chill the pie overnight, or for at least 6 hours.

5. Cut the pie into slices and serve. Store any leftovers in the refrigerator, covered with plastic wrap or foil, for up to 3 days.

Get creative with decorating your pie: Add a drizzle of chocolate syrup, chocolate shavings, crushed-up Oreo cookies, or chocolate sprinkles on top, if you like.

105 DESSERTS & DOG TREAT

YOU'LL WANT S'MORE, S'MORES DIP

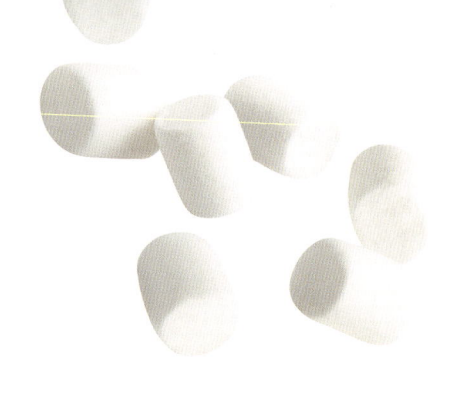

Milk chocolate chips are topped with a layer of marshmallows, then baked until the chocolate is melty and the marshmallows are toasty. Scoop the gooey, delicious dip onto graham crackers for a fun (and a little bit messy!) treat.

SERVES 4

PREP TIME
5 minutes

COOK TIME
10 minutes

INGREDIENTS

- Cooking oil spray, such as avocado oil
- 1 ½ cups (10 ounces) milk chocolate chips
- 4 cups (about 7 ounces) mini marshmallows

FOR SERVING

- Graham crackers

You can substitute white chocolate or dark chocolate chips for the milk chocolate ones, and dip any cookies you like. Shortbread, digestive biscuits, butter cookies, or any other sturdy cookie works well.

DIRECTIONS

1 Preheat the oven to 375°F with an oven rack in the middle position. Spray a small (8 x 8–inch or 6 x 9–inch) baking dish with cooking spray.

2 Place the chocolate chips in a single layer in the baking dish, then top them with the mini marshmallows.

3 Place the baking dish on a baking sheet and bake for about 10 minutes, or until the marshmallows are puffed up and lightly toasted, and the chocolate has melted. Serve warm, with graham crackers on the side. This should be eaten right away—the chocolate will harden as it cools.

107 DESSERTS & DOG TREAT

FUNFETTI COOKIES

A store-bought package of sugar cookie dough and some sprinkles make these easy cookies festive and fun. Kids of any age can shape the cookie dough into balls and roll them in the sprinkles.

CLYDEO'S TIPS AND TRICKS

Use whatever color sprinkles you like for this recipe! Red and green Christmas sprinkles, rainbow sprinkles for a birthday, orange and black for Halloween, red and pink for Valentine's Day.

MAKES 24 COOKIES

PREP TIME
10 minutes
(plus 10 minutes to cool)

COOK TIME
8 minutes

INGREDIENTS

- ⅔ cup rainbow sprinkles
- 1 (16-ounce) package sugar cookie dough (24 break-apart cookies)

DIRECTIONS

1. Preheat the oven to 350°F with an oven rack in the middle position. Line two baking sheets with parchment paper.

2. Pour the sprinkles into a shallow bowl.

3. Break the cookie dough into 24 pieces. Roll the dough pieces into round balls, roll them in the sprinkles, and then place them on the prepared baking sheets.

4. Bake the cookies for 12 to 14 minutes, or until they are a light golden brown around the edges.

5. Let the cookies cool on the pans for 2 minutes, then using a thin, flexible spatula, transfer them to a cooling rack. Let cool to room temperature (or for at least 10 minutes) and then enjoy.

NOTE The cookies can be stored in a tightly lidded container on the counter for up to 1 week, or in the freezer for up to 3 months.

109 DESSERTS & DOG TREAT

CARAMEL APPLE PRETZEL BITES

Each mini pretzel is topped with a melted caramel and a slice of tart apple for a delicious one-bite dessert. I love this sweet and salty treat that's easy and fun to make!

MAKES ABOUT 36 BITES

PREP TIME
10 minutes
(plus 10 minutes to cool)

COOK TIME
5 minutes

INGREDIENTS

- 3 large granny smith or other tart, crisp apples
- 36 butter snap pretzels (the square, bite-size ones) or any mini pretzels
- 1 (11-ounce) bag (36) Kraft caramels, unwrapped

DIRECTIONS

1. Preheat the oven to 350°F with an oven rack in the middle position. Line a baking sheet with parchment paper.

2. Core and quarter the three apples. Slice each quarter into three wedges, to make 36 pieces of apple.

3. Spread out a single layer of pretzels on the prepared baking sheet, then top each one with a piece of caramel. Bake for about 5 minutes, or until the caramel just begins to soften and melt but isn't melting off the pretzels.

4. Remove the bites from the oven and immediately top each one with a piece of apple, pushing the apple into the caramel so it sticks on top.

5. Let the bites cool for 10 minutes, transfer to serving plates, and enjoy right away.

NOTE: Drizzle some melted chocolate on top of these for an even more decadent bite. Add sprinkles or chopped nuts if you like, too!

111   DESSERTS & DOG TREAT

SCRUMPTIOUS STRAWBERRY & CHEESECAKE ICE CREAM SANDWICHES

I love to combine my favorite treats to make a decadent dessert. Cheesecake meets ice cream in these sweet and tangy sandwiches. Mix together the whipped topping and whipped cream cheese for a fluffy and soft filling.

MAKES 12 SANDWICHES

PREP TIME
15 minutes
(plus 4 hours to chill)

INGREDIENTS

- 12 graham cracker sheets
- 1 (8-ounce) tub Cool Whip
- 1 (8-ounce) container whipped cream cheese, room temperature
- ½ cup powdered sugar, sifted
- 1 cup chopped fresh strawberries

DIRECTIONS

1. Break the graham cracker sheets in half to make squares. Arrange half the squares in a single layer in an 8 x 8–inch baking dish.

2. In a medium bowl, combine the Cool Whip and cream cheese. Using a hand mixer, blend them together for about 1 minute at medium-high speed, or until smooth and well combined. Add the sugar and chopped strawberries and stir, using a rubber spatula, until evenly combined.

3. Spoon the whipped topping mixture onto the graham crackers, then cover with the remaining graham cracker squares.

4. Cover the dish with plastic wrap and freeze for at least 4 hours, or until firm. Slice into squares and enjoy!

NOTE Bananas work well in place of the strawberries, and they give banana pudding vibes to this dessert treat.

CLYDEO'S TIPS AND TRICKS

If you forgot to soften your cream cheese ahead of time, place the unopened tub in a bowl of hot water for 10 minutes and it will soften right up.

113   DESSERTS & DOG TREAT

NO-BAKE CRISPY RICE PEANUT BUTTER BARS

I am just nuts for peanut butter, aren't you? If so, you'll surely want to devour these yummy bars. Use crunchy peanut butter for extra texture!

CLYDEO'S TIPS AND TRICKS

Anytime you're working with marshmallows, things are going to get messy! Here are some tips to keep things slightly less gooey: Line your baking dish with parchment paper, leaving an overhang around the edges of the pan; these will serve as handles to lift out the cooled treats. Spray your spatula with cooking spray before stirring the marshmallow mixture. To avoid getting gooey mallow stuck on your paws, wet them with water, shaking off any excess before touching the mixture. Finally, spray down the knife with cooking spray before using it to cut the bars.

MAKES 12 BARS

PREP TIME
10 minutes
(plus 1 hour to cool)

COOK TIME
10 minutes

INGREDIENTS

- 3 tablespoons unsalted butter, plus more for greasing the pan
- 1 (12-ounce) package marshmallows
- ½ cup peanut butter (crunchy or smooth)
- 6 cups puffed rice cereal
- ¼ cup mini M&M's, chocolate chips, or chopped peanuts

NOTE For extra-thick bars, use an 8 x 8-inch pan instead of a 9 x 13-inch.

114

DESSERTS & DOG TREAT

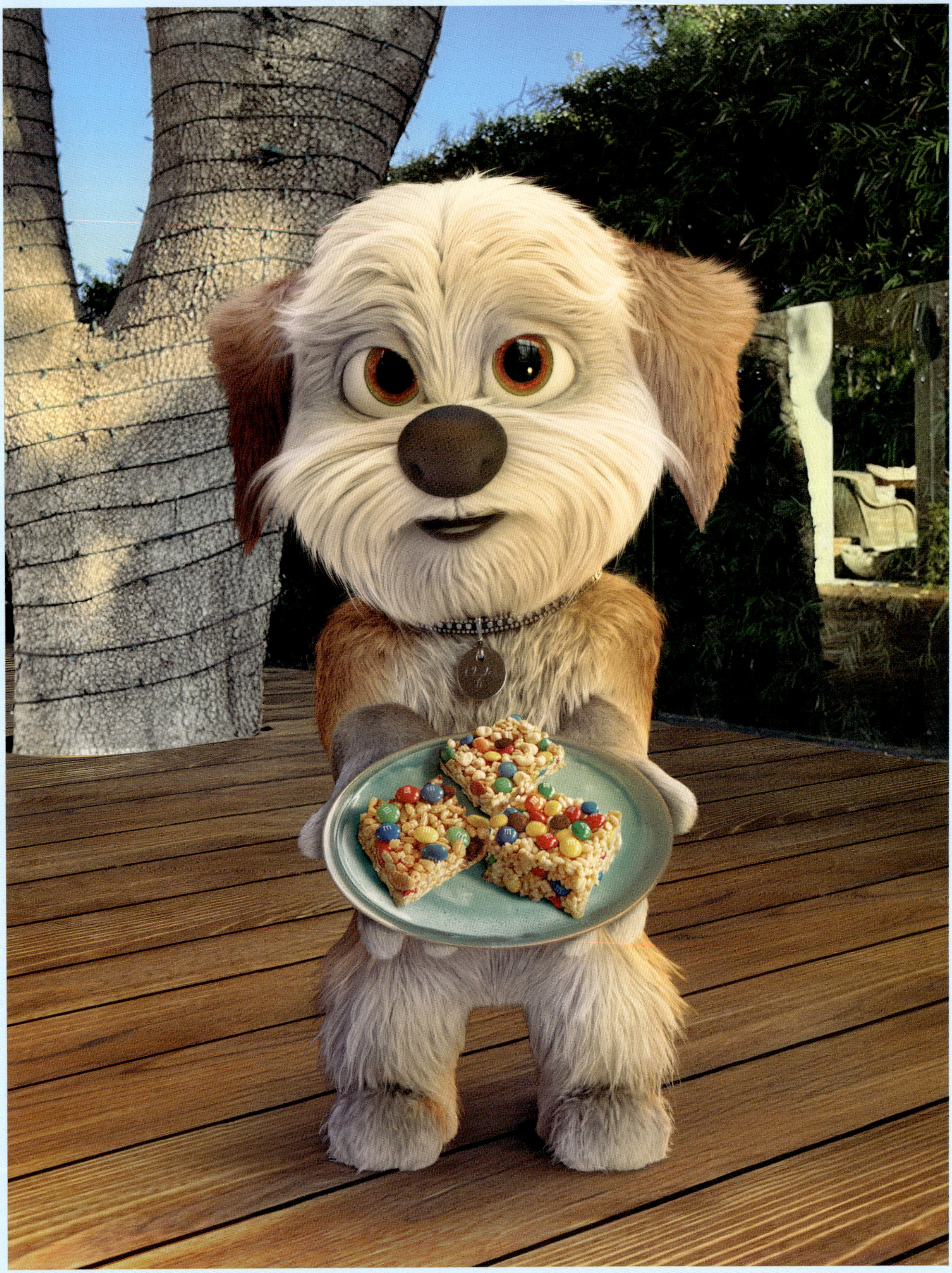

NO-BAKE CRISPY RICE PEANUT BUTTER BARS

DIRECTIONS

1. Grease a 9 x13–inch baking pan with butter.

2. In a large saucepan, melt the butter over medium-low heat. Stir in the marshmallows and let them melt, stirring continuously for about 5 minutes, or until the mixture is completely smooth. Turn off the heat, then stir in the peanut butter until fully incorporated.

3. Stir in the puffed rice cereal until it's completely coated in the marshmallow/peanut butter mixture.

4. Transfer the mixture to the prepared baking pan. Place a sheet of parchment or wax paper over the mixture, then using a spoon or spatula, press down the mixture into an even layer.

5. Remove the parchment, sprinkle the M&M's over the top while the mixture is still warm, place the parchment back over the mixture, and press them in.

6. Let cool for 1 hour, then slice into bars and serve.

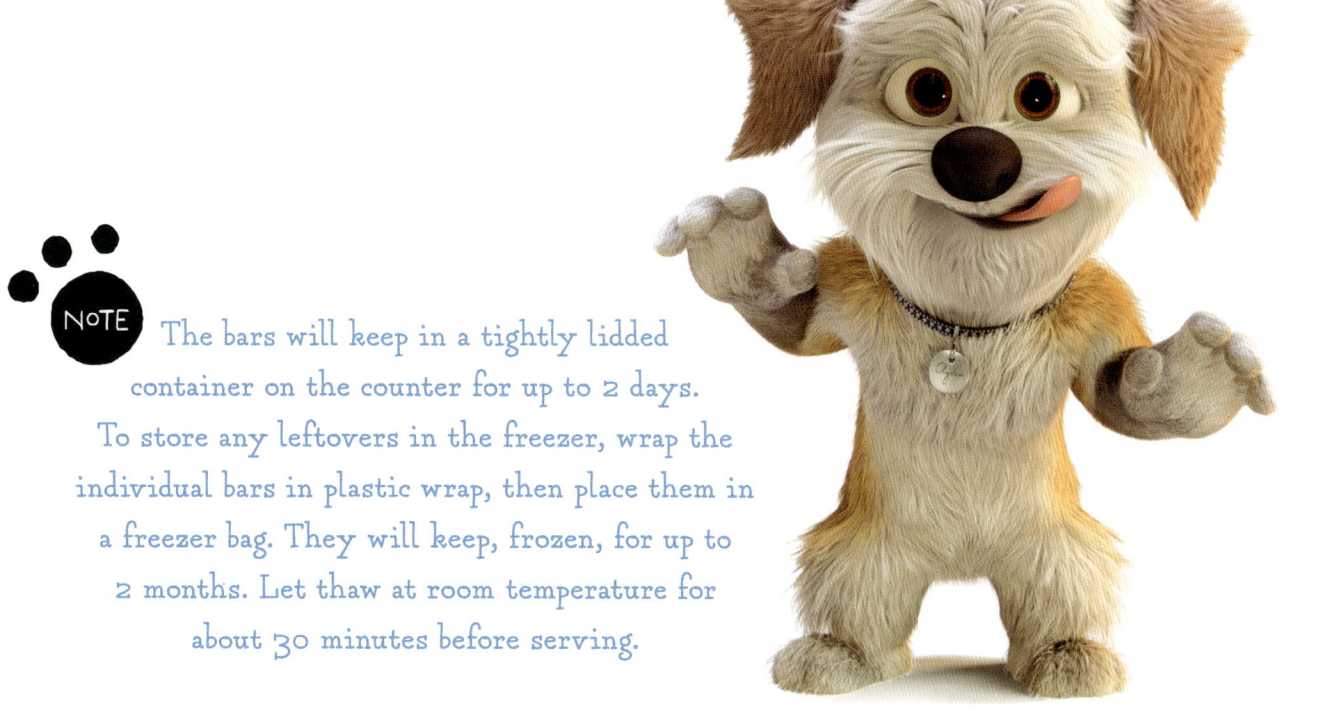

NOTE The bars will keep in a tightly lidded container on the counter for up to 2 days. To store any leftovers in the freezer, wrap the individual bars in plastic wrap, then place them in a freezer bag. They will keep, frozen, for up to 2 months. Let thaw at room temperature for about 30 minutes before serving.

DESSERTS & DOG TREAT

4-INGREDIENT HOMEMADE DOG TREATS

Finally, a homemade treat that your furry friends can enjoy! Banana, peanut butter, oats, and a dash of cinnamon make these irresistible to any dog. Substitute pureed pumpkin for the banana for a fall treat.

MAKES 12 TREATS

PREP TIME
10 minutes
(plus 20 minutes to cool)

COOK TIME
10 minutes

INGREDIENTS

- 1 ripe medium banana
- ½ cup natural (no salt added) peanut butter
- ½ teaspoon ground cinnamon
- 1 cup old-fashioned rolled oats

Check the ingredients on your peanut butter to make sure it's safe for dogs. If it contains xylitol, it's not safe for your furry friends. For the safest, healthiest option, choose a natural, "no salt added" variety that contains just peanuts.

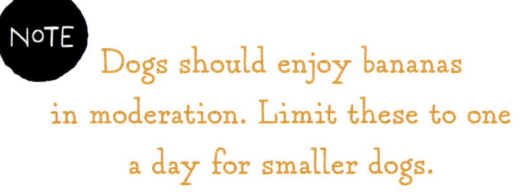

NOTE Dogs should enjoy bananas in moderation. Limit these to one a day for smaller dogs.

DESSERTS & DOG TREAT

These dog treats will keep, stored in a tightly lidded container, in the refrigerator for up to a week or the freezer for up to 2 months.

4-INGREDIENT HOMEMADE DOG TREATS

DIRECTIONS

1 Preheat the oven to 350°F with an oven rack in the middle position. Line a baking sheet with parchment paper.

2 In a large mixing bowl, using a fork, mash the banana until no large lumps remain. Stir in the peanut butter and cinnamon, then stir in the oats.

3 Using a 1 ½-tablespoon (small) cookie scoop, portion the mixture onto the prepared baking sheet. Get your fingers a little wet, then press each treat down into a ¼–inch-thick circle.

4 Bake the treats for about 10 minutes, or until they're lightly brown. Transfer to a cooling rack and let cool completely before giving to your dog.

DESSERTS & DOG TREAT

Bone appétit!